family circle®

quick and easy

CAKES

The Family Circle® Promise of Success

Welcome to the world of Confident Cooking, created for you in the Australian **Family Circle® Test Kitchen,** where recipes are double-tested by our team of home economists to achieve a high standard of success—and delicious results every time.

MURDOCH
BOOKS

All recipes are double-tested by our team of home economists. When we test our recipes, we rate them for ease of preparation. The following cookery ratings are on the recipes in this book, making them easy to use and understand.

A single Cooking with Confidence symbol indicates a recipe that is simple and generally quick to make—perfect for beginners.

Two symbols indicate the need for just a little more care and a little more time.

Three symbols indicate special dishes that need more investment in time, care and patience—but the results are worth it.

TEST KITCHEN PERFECTION

You'll never make a wrong move with a Family Circle® step-by-step cookbook. Our team of home economists has tested and refined the recipes so that you can create fabulous food in your own kitchen. Follow our easy instructions and step-by-step photographs and you'll feel like there is a master chef in the kitchen guiding you every step of the way.

IMPORTANT

Those who might be at risk from the effects of salmonella food poisoning (the elderly, pregnant women, young children and those suffering from immune deficiency diseases) should consult their GP with any concerns about eating raw eggs.

The Publisher thanks: Chief Australia; Breville Holdings Pty Ltd; Kambrook; Bertolli Olive Oil; Southcorp Appliances; Sheldon & Hammond.

Front cover: *Tiramisu cake, page 97.*
Inside front cover: *Praline butter cake, page 106 (top), and Butterfly cupcakes, page 31.*
Back cover: *Rich dark chocolate cake, page 68.*

CONTENTS

Top: *Orange flower sponge, page 95.*
Bottom left: *Chocolate cherry cake, page 80.* **Bottom right:** *Chestnut cake, page 55.*

CAKES THE EASY WAY

Who said you can't have your cake and eat it too? With a cake for all occasions, this book dispells the myth of tedious preparation and lengthy ingredient lists to achieve a masterpiece—the following tips and techniques show you how.

This book is divided into four chapters: Beat and mix cakes, Melt and mix cakes, Food processor cakes and Dressed up packet cakes. To give you more time to 'eat your cake', we have limited the preparation time to 15 minutes or less, and kept the ingredient list to no more than eight items.

Not all the cakes have an icing or topping included in the recipe. We have also provided a separate icings section with a range of buttercreams, icings, glazes and a ganache or two, for you to refer to. Follow our suggestions or mix and match your own favourites.

The packet cake chapter shows how eight ingredients can transform a packet cake into a showstopper, such as tiramisu cake or the perennial favourite; Black Forest cake. It's important that you buy the correct weight cake mix so your cake will fit in the tin. We have included the ingredients that it needs in the ingredients list so there is no need to follow the directions on the packet. The method is also included so all you need to do is empty the contents into a bowl and follow the recipe. It's that simple.

When you start to make your cake, it is very important to read through the recipe first to ensure you have all the necessary ingredients and equipment. Preheat the oven to the appropriate temperature and place the cake on the middle shelf once it has reached the correct temperature.

Cake tins are greased and lined to prevent the mixture sticking to the tin. Always prepare the tin according to the instructions before preparing the cake (see facing page).

GREASING AND LINING THE TIN

Grease the tin using melted unsalted butter or a mild-flavoured oil. Apply just enough to evenly coat the base and side(s) of the tin using a pastry brush, making sure there is no excess dripping back to the base of the tin—oil sprays are a quick and easy alternative (spray away from the heat source in a well-ventilated area).

Greaseproof paper is the preferred baking paper for lining cake tins.

LINING A ROUND CAKE TIN

Step 1: If lining the side of a round tin, cut a strip of baking paper long enough to cover the outside of the tin and up to 6 cm wider than the height. Fold down a 2 cm cuff, then cut the cuff on the diagonal at 2 cm intervals.

Step 2: Grease the base and side of the tin and place the strip of baking paper against the inside of the tin with the cut cuff sitting neatly on the base—the cut cuff will act like pleats.

Step 3: Place the cake tin on a sheet of baking paper and trace around the outside, then cut out with a pair of scissors. Place, pencil-side down, onto the base of the tin over the pleats and smooth out any bubbles. If just lining the base, complete step 3 only.

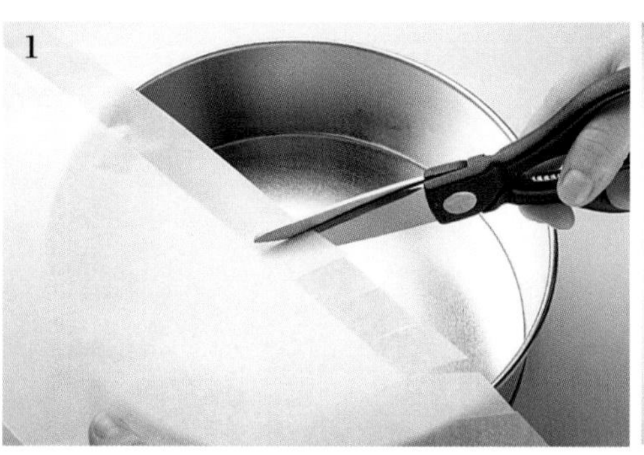

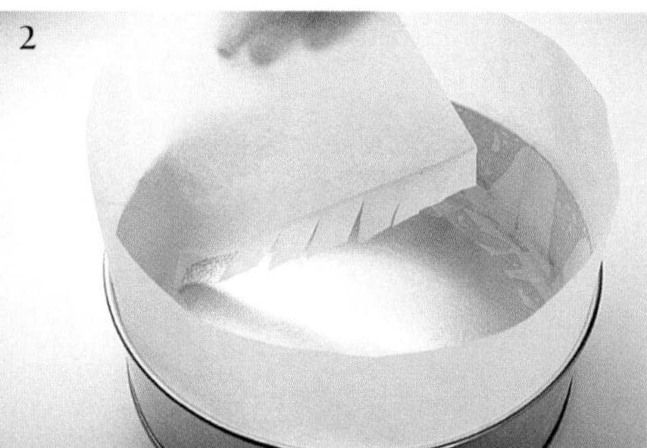

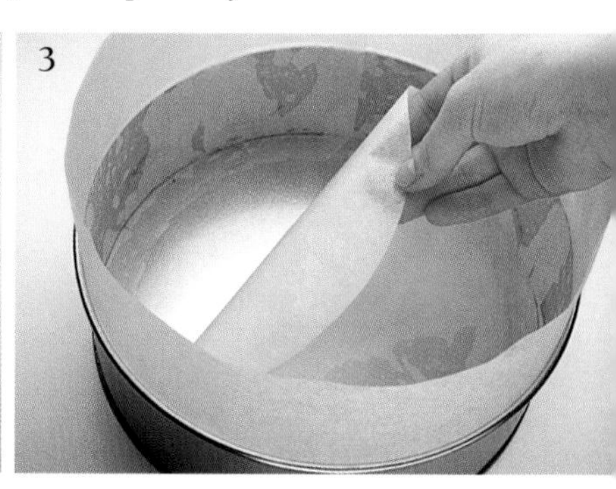

LINING A SQUARE CAKE TIN

Step 1: Place the cake tin on a sheet of baking paper and trace around the outside with a pencil.

Step 2: Cut out the baking paper with a pair of scissors and place, pencil-side down, onto the base of the tin, smoothing out any air bubbles.

Step 3: If lining the sides of the tin as well, cut a strip of baking paper the same length as the outside of the tin and 1 cm wider than the height. Place against the inside around the sides, smoothing out any bubbles.

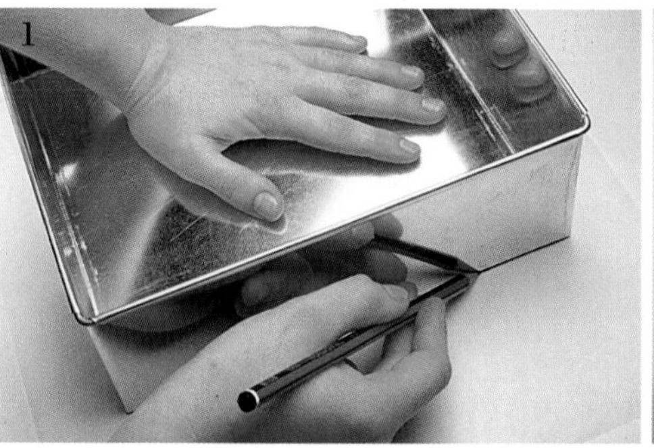

MEASURING EQUIPMENT

- Use metric measuring cups for dry ingredients such as flour and sugar. Place the measuring cup on a flat surface and lightly spoon in the ingredients. Level off the surface with a flat-bladed knife—do not shake or tap the cup. To measure soft brown sugar, pack down firmly (unless 'lightly packed' is specified), then level off the surface.
- Metric measuring jugs are used for liquid ingredients, such as milk or water. Place the jug on a flat surface, add the liquid and check the measured markings at eye level for an accurate reading.
- Measuring spoons are used to measure small amounts of dry and liquid ingredients. They are usually sold in sets of 1/4 teaspoon, 1/2 teaspoon, 1 teaspoon (5 ml) and 1 tablespoon (20 ml).
- Kitchen scales are useful when measuring ingredients such as nuts, chocolate and butter. Some blocks of butter have gram weight markings on the wrapper, but these can be inaccurate if wrapped unevenly

PANTRY EQUIPMENT

- Electric beaters reduce the preparation time when making cakes, by effortlessly creaming butter and sugar mixtures to the correct consistency, beating egg whites till soft or stiff peaks form and beating egg white mixtures quickly and easily.
- Food processors are ideal for blending ingredients together and we have dedicated a whole chapter to this method of making cakes. However, only use a food processor when specified, as this technique is not always suitable, particularly for methods such as creaming.
- Check the size of your cake tin by measuring the diameter or width and length of the base. It is important to use the tin size specified in the recipe or at least one of the same cup capacity—check by measuring with water. Aluminium tins give consistently good results. Avoid using dark-coloured tins as they can brown the cake before it cooks.

ICINGS

WHITE CHOCOLATE CREAM CHEESE ICING

100 g white chocolate
1/4 cup (60 ml) cream
200 g cream cheese, softened
1/3 cup (40 g) icing sugar

Melt the chocolate and cream in a small saucepan over low heat until smooth. Cool slightly, add to the cream cheese and icing sugar and beat until smooth.

ORANGE CREAM CHEESE FROSTING

60 g cream cheese, softened
20 g unsalted butter, softened
1 teaspoon grated orange rind
2 teaspoons orange juice
1 cup (125 g) icing sugar, sifted

Beat the cream cheese, butter, rind and juice in a bowl with electric beaters until light and fluffy. Gradually beat in the icing sugar until smooth.

LEMON CREAM CHEESE ICING

60 g cream cheese, softened
30 g unsalted butter, softened
1 tablespoon lemon juice
1 1/2 cups (185 g) icing sugar, sifted

Beat the cream cheese and butter in a small bowl. Add the lemon juice and sugar and beat until smooth.

PASSIONFRUIT ICING

1 1/4 cups (155 g) icing sugar, sifted
10 g unsalted butter, softened
1/4 cup (60 ml) passionfruit pulp

Combine the icing sugar, butter and enough passionfruit pulp in a small bowl to make a stiff paste. Stand the bowl in a saucepan of simmering water, stirring until the icing is smooth and glossy. Remove the bowl from the heat. Spread the icing over the cake with a flat-bladed knife and allow to set before serving.

COFFEE BUTTERCREAM

3 teaspoons instant coffee powder
125 g unsalted butter, softened
1 1/2 cups (185 g) icing sugar, sifted
1/2 teaspoon vanilla essence
2 teaspoons milk

Dissolve the coffee in 2 tablespoons boiling water. Beat the butter and icing sugar with electric beaters until pale and creamy. Add the vanilla, coffee mixture and milk and beat for 2 minutes, or until smooth and fluffy.

MOCHA GANACHE

1 tablespoon instant coffee powder
100 g dark chocolate, chopped
1/3 cup (80 ml) cream

Dissolve the coffee powder in 2 teaspoons boiling water. Place the chocolate and cream with the coffee mixture in a small saucepan. Stir over low heat until the chocolate has melted and the mixture is smooth. Remove from the heat, cool slightly and pour over the cake.

RICOTTA HONEY ICING

1 1/2 cups (375 g) smooth ricotta
70 g unsalted butter, softened
2 tablespoons honey

Beat the ricotta, butter and honey with electric beaters for 2–3 minutes, or until light and creamy. Spread over the top and sides of the cake to cover.
This icing will not keep well due to the water content of the ricotta.

COFFEE GLACE ICING

1 cup (125 g) icing sugar, sifted
1 teaspoon instant coffee powder
10 g unsalted butter, softened

Combine the icing sugar, coffee powder, butter and 1–2 tablespoons of water to form a firm paste in a small heatproof bowl. Stand the bowl over a saucepan of simmering water and stir until smooth and glossy. Remove from the heat. Spread the icing over the cake with a spatula.

CHOCOLATE GANACHE

150 g dark chocolate, chopped
1/4 cup (60 ml) cream

Combine the chocolate and cream in a small saucepan. Stir over low heat until the chocolate has melted and the mixture is smooth. Remove from the heat and allow to cool. Pour the ganache on to the cake, then smooth the top and around the side with a flat-bladed knife.

LEMON GLACE ICING

1 cup (125 g) icing sugar, sifted
1 teaspoon grated lemon rind
10 g unsalted butter, softened
1–2 tablespoons lemon juice

Combine the sifted icing sugar, lemon rind, butter and enough of the juice to form a firm paste in a small heatproof bowl. Stand the bowl over a saucepan of simmering water and stir until the icing is smooth and glossy. Remove from the heat. Spread the icing over the cake using a wide knife.

CHOCOLATE FUDGE ICING

150 g dark chocolate, coarsely chopped
90 g unsalted butter, chopped
1/2 cup (160 g) condensed milk

Combine the chocolate, butter and condensed milk in a small saucepan. Stir over low heat until the chocolate and butter have melted and the mixture is smooth. Remove from the heat. Allow to cool until thick and spreadable.

ORANGE GLACE ICING

1 cup (125 g) icing sugar, sifted
10 g unsalted butter, softened
1 teaspoon grated orange rind
2 tablespoons orange juice

Combine the icing sugar, butter, grated rind and enough of the juice to make a soft pouring consistency. Stand the bowl over a saucepan of simmering water and stir until the icing is smooth and glossy. Remove from the heat. Drizzle over the cake and let it run down the sides.

LIME ICING

2 cups (250 g) icing sugar, sifted
80 g unsalted butter, softened
2 tablespoons lime juice

Place the icing sugar, butter and lime juice in a bowl and beat with a wooden spoon until smooth, adding 1–2 tablespoons water, if necessary. Spread over the cake with a flat-bladed knife.

GINGER ICING

80 g butter
1 tablespoon golden syrup
3/4 cup (90 g) icing sugar
1 teaspoon ground ginger

Mix the butter, syrup, icing sugar and ginger in a saucepan over low heat. Stir often, bring just to the boil then remove from the heat. Spread over the cake with a flat-bladed knife.

CARAMEL ICING

1 1/2 cups (185 g) icing sugar
1 tablespoon milk
2 tablespoons golden syrup
30 g unsalted butter, softened

Place the icing sugar, milk, golden syrup and butter in a bowl and beat with a wooden spoon until smooth. Spread over the cake with a flat-bladed knife.

COCONUT ICING

60 g butter, softened
few drops coconut essence
3/4 cup (90 g) icing sugar, sifted
1 tablespoon milk

Place the butter and coconut essence in a small bowl and beat with electric beaters until light and creamy. Add the icing sugar and milk and beat until the mixture is light and fluffy.

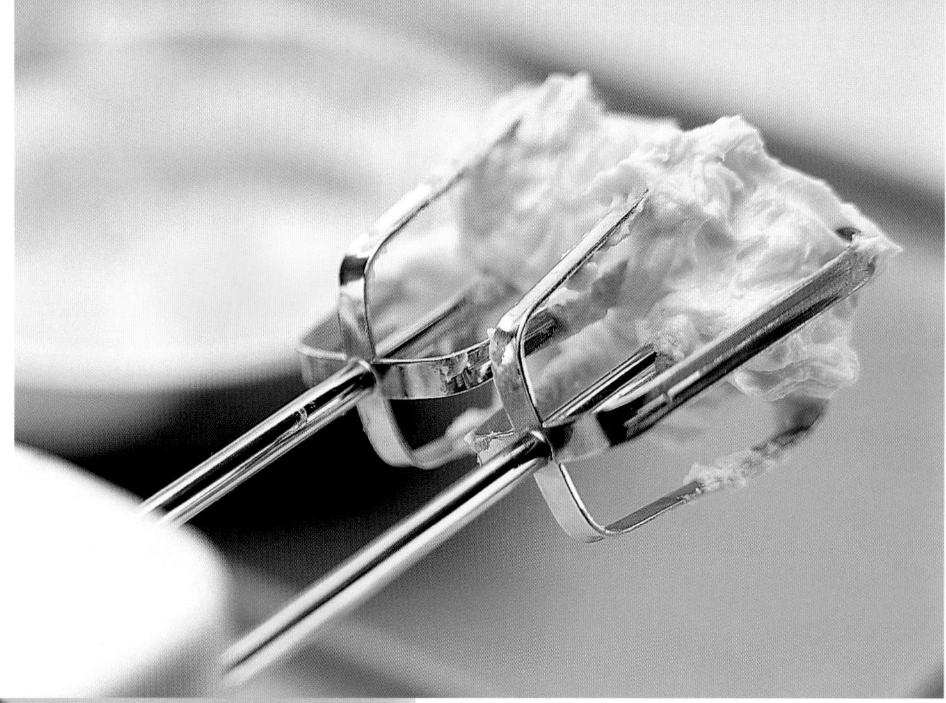

WHITE CHOCOLATE GANACHE

150 g white chocolate melts
130 g white chocolate, chopped
1/2 cup (125 ml) cream
250 g unsalted butter, chopped

Place the white chocolate melts, white chocolate, cream and butter in a saucepan and stir over low heat until both the chocolate and butter have melted and the mixture is smooth. Transfer to a bowl, cover the surface with plastic wrap and leave to cool completely—do not refrigerate. Beat with electric beaters for 3–5 minutes, or until thick, pale and creamy.

HONEY AND CREAM CHEESE ICING

125 g cream cheese, softened
1/2 cup (60 g) icing sugar, sifted
1 tablespoon honey

Place the cream cheese in a bowl and beat with electric beaters until creamy. Add the icing sugar and honey, then beat for 3 minutes, or until smooth and fluffy. Spread the icing over the cake with a flat-bladed knife.

CHOCOLATE GLAZE

50 g dark chocolate, finely chopped
25 g unsalted butter, chopped
1/4 cup (30 g) icing sugar, sifted
2 teaspoons cream

Place the chocolate, butter, icing sugar and cream in a small saucepan. Stir over low heat until the mixture is smooth and glossy. Remove from the heat and spread on the cake with a spatula.

GINGER AND LEMON GLACE ICING

1/3 cup (40 g) icing sugar, sifted
1/2 teaspoon ground ginger
20 g unsalted butter, melted
2 teaspoons milk
1 teaspoon lemon juice

Combine the icing sugar, ground ginger, butter, milk and lemon juice in a bowl to form a paste. Place over a saucepan of simmering water, stirring until the icing is smooth and glossy. Remove the bowl from the heat. Drizzle the icing over the cake or spread, working quickly, with a knife dipped in hot water for even covering. Do not reheat the icing.

PINEAPPLE ICING

1 1/2 cups (185 g) icing sugar, sifted
2 tablespoons pineapple juice
2 teaspoons unsalted butter

Combine the icing sugar, pineapple juice and butter in a small heatproof bowl. Stand the bowl in a saucepan of simmering water, stirring until the butter has melted and the icing is glossy and smooth. Cool slightly. Drizzle the icing over the cake with a spoon.

HONEY FROSTING

90 g cream cheese, softened
2 teaspoons honey
1 teaspoon finely grated lemon rind
1 1/2 cups (185 g) icing sugar, sifted

Place the cream cheese, honey and lemon rind in a bowl and beat with electric beaters until light and creamy. Add the icing sugar and beat for a further 3–4 minutes, or until smooth and fluffy.

BUTTERSCOTCH FROSTING

20 g unsalted butter, chopped
1/2 cup (95 g) lightly packed soft brown sugar
1/3 cup (90 g) sour cream
100 g cream cheese, softened

Place the butter and brown sugar in a small saucepan. Stir constantly over low heat until it boils and the sugar dissolves. Simmer for 3 minutes, stirring occasionally. Remove from the heat, add the sour cream and stir until combined. Cool. Beat the cream cheese with electric beaters until light and creamy. Gradually add the cooled butterscotch mixture, beating well after each addition.

CREAMY APRICOT TOPPING

1/3 cup (60 g) finely chopped dried apricots
100 g cream cheese, softened
2 tablespoons icing sugar, sifted

Place the apricots and 1/2 cup (125 ml) water in a small saucepan. Stir over high heat until the mixture boils. Reduce the heat, simmer without stirring, for 10 minutes, or until almost all the liquid is absorbed and the apricots are soft. Remove from the heat and cool completely. Beat the cream cheese and icing sugar with electric beaters until light and creamy. Add the undrained apricot pulp, beating for 2 minutes, or until fluffy and almost smooth.

BEAT AND MIX CAKES

HAWAIIAN MACADAMIA CAKE

Preparation time: 10 minutes
Total cooking time: 1 hour 15 minutes
Serves 10–12

- 3 cups (375 g) self-raising flour
- 1 teaspoon ground cinnamon
- 1 1/2 cups (375 g) caster sugar
- 1 cup (90 g) desiccated coconut
- 5 eggs, lightly beaten
- 440 g can crushed pineapple in syrup
- 1 1/2 cups (375 ml) vegetable oil
- 100 g macadamia nuts, chopped

1 Preheat the oven to moderate 180°C (350°F/Gas 4). Grease a 23 cm round deep cake tin. Line the base and side with two sheets of baking paper, cutting it to sit 2–3 cm above the side of the tin. Sift the flour and cinnamon into a large bowl, add the sugar and coconut and stir to combine. Add the eggs, pineapple and oil and mix well. Stir in the macadamia nuts.

2 Spoon the mixture into the prepared tin and level the surface. Bake for 1 hour 15 minutes, or until a skewer comes out clean when inserted into the centre of the cake—cover with foil if it browns too much. Leave in the tin for 30 minutes before turning out onto a wire rack.

NUTRITION PER SERVE (12)
Fat 42.5 g; Protein 7 g; Carbohydrate 59 g; Dietary Fibre 3.5 g; Cholesterol 75 mg; 2650 kJ (635 cal)

COOK'S FILE
Note: Top with Lemon cream cheese icing (see page 6).

1

2

DATE CHOCOLATE TORTE

Preparation time: 15 minutes
Total cooking time: 35 minutes
Serves 6

100 g slivered almonds
120 g dark chocolate, coarsely chopped
120 g dried dates, pitted
3 egg whites
1/2 cup (125 g) caster sugar
1/2 cup (125 ml) cream
2 teaspoons caster sugar, extra
30 g dark chocolate, grated, extra

1 Preheat the oven to moderate 180°C (350°F/Gas 4). Grease a 22 cm springform tin and line with foil. Chop the almonds and chocolate in a food processor until fine. Finely chop the dates with a sharp knife.
2 Beat the egg whites with electric beaters until soft peaks form. Slowly add the sugar and continue beating until it dissolves. Fold in the almond and chocolate mixture, then the dates. Spoon the mixture into the prepared tin and level the surface. Bake for 30–35 minutes, or until set and it starts to come away from the side. Cool in the tin before carefully turning out onto a serving plate.
To serve, whip the cream and extra sugar until soft peaks form. Spread the cream evenly over the top with a spatula. Sprinkle with the grated chocolate to decorate.

NUTRITION PER SERVE
Fat 25.5 g; Protein 7 g; Carbohydrate 52.5 g; Dietary Fibre 4 g; Cholesterol 28.5 mg; 1905 kJ (455 cal)

COOK'S FILE
Note: This is great served for a special afternoon tea, or as a dessert.
Storage: This torte keeps well, without cream, for 5–6 days wrapped in foil. With cream, this is best served the day after baking.

1

2

CHERRY FRUITCAKE

Preparation time: 10 minutes
Total cooking time: 2 hours
Serves 8–10

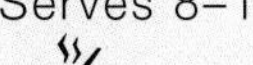

- 1 1/4 cups (155 g) self-raising flour
- 1 cup (250 g) sugar
- 1/2 cup (125 ml) orange juice concentrate
- 4 eggs
- 450 g roasted and peeled hazelnuts
- 400 g pitted dates, chopped
- 2 x 250 g jars maraschino cherries, well drained

1 Preheat the oven to slow 150°C (300°F/Gas 2). Grease a 22 x 12 cm loaf tin and line the base and sides with baking paper, then layer another two times to make three layers in total, greasing between each layer. Sift the flour into a large bowl and add the sugar, orange juice concentrate, eggs and 1 teaspoon salt. Mix well.

2 Stir in the hazelnuts, dates and all but 10 of the cherries. The mixture will be quite thin.

3 Pour into the prepared tin. Cut the remaining cherries in half and arrange in three flower designs down the centre of the cake. Bake for 2 hours, or until a skewer comes out clean when inserted into the centre of the cake. Cool in the tin before turning out onto a wire rack.

NUTRITION PER SERVE (10)
Fat 30 g; Protein 12 g; Carbohydrate 79 g; Dietary Fibre 8.5 g; Cholesterol 72 mg; 2595 kJ (620 cal)

1

2

3

EASY FRUITCAKE

Preparation time: 10 minutes
Total cooking time: 2 hours 10 minutes
Serves 6–8

3 eggs
1/2 cup (125 ml) milk
410 g jar mincemeat
3/4 cup (185 g) caster sugar
2 cups (375 g) mixed fruit
1 cup (125 g) chopped walnuts
2 1/2 cups (310 g) plain flour
1 teaspoon baking soda

1 Preheat the oven to slow 150°C (300°F/Gas 2). Grease a deep 23 cm round cake tin and line the base and side with 3–4 layers of baking paper.
2 Beat the eggs, milk, mincemeat, sugar, mixed fruit and walnuts in a large bowl until combined. Sift in the flour and baking soda and mix well.
3 Spoon into the prepared tin and bake for 2 hours 10 minutes, or until a skewer comes out clean when inserted into the centre of the cake. Cool in the tin for 15 minutes. Turn out and cool on a wire rack. Wrap well in foil and store for up to 2 weeks.

NUTRITION PER SERVE (8)
Fat 15.5 g; Protein 11 g; Carbohydrate 99 g; Dietary Fibre 6.5 g; Cholesterol 70.5 mg; 2380 kJ (570 cal)

COOK'S FILE
Note: If desired, spread with an orange glaze—place 2 tablespoons apricot jam in a saucepan with 2 tablespoons hot water. Stir over low heat until melted and combined. Strain through a strainer. Brush the mixture over the top of the cake with a pastry brush.

1

2

3

ZUCCHINI AND WALNUT CAKE

Preparation time: 12 minutes
Total cooking time: 1 hour 10 minutes
Serves 6–8

- 2 1/2 cups (245 g) walnuts
- 500 g zucchini
- 1 cup (250 ml) canola oil
- 1 1/2 cups (330 g) raw sugar
- 3 eggs
- 2 1/2 cups (310 g) self-raising flour, sifted
- 1 1/2 teaspoons ground cinnamon
- 1 teaspoon ground nutmeg

1 Preheat the oven to warm 170°C (325°F/Gas 3). Grease a 22 x 12 cm loaf tin and line the base and two long sides with a sheet of baking paper. Roughly chop 185 g of the walnuts. Grate the zucchini. Place the zucchini in a large bowl with the oil, sugar, eggs and chopped walnuts and mix well. Stir in the flour, cinnamon and nutmeg.

2 Spoon the mixture into the tin and arrange the remaining walnuts on top. Bake for 1 hour 10 minutes, or until a skewer comes out clean when inserted into the centre of the cake. Leave in the tin for 20 minutes before turning out onto a wire rack to cool. Cut into slices and serve.

NUTRITION PER SERVE (8)
Fat 52.5 g; Protein 11 g; Carbohydrate 71 g; Dietary Fibre 4.5 g; Cholesterol 67.5 mg; 3300 kJ (790 cal)

COOK'S FILE
Storage: Wrap in foil when cooled. the cake will keep for 4–5 days.

1

2

MADEIRA CAKE

Preparation time: 10 minutes
Total cooking time: 1 hour
Serves 6

180 g unsalted butter, softened
3/4 cup (185 g) caster sugar
3 eggs, beaten
1 1/3 cups (165 g) self-raising flour, sifted
2 teaspoons finely grated lemon rind
1 teaspoon lemon juice
2 teaspoons caster sugar, extra, for sprinkling

1 Preheat the oven to warm 160°C (315°F/Gas 2–3). Grease and flour a deep 18 cm round cake tin, shaking out any excess. Beat the butter and sugar with electric beaters until pale and creamy. Add the eggs gradually, beating well after each addition. Fold in the flour, lemon rind and juice until combined. When smooth, spoon into the prepared tin and level the surface.

2 Sprinkle the extra sugar over the top. Bake for 1 hour, or until a skewer comes out clean when inserted into the centre of the cake. Cool for 15 minutes in the tin before turning out onto a wire rack to cool. If desired, dust with icing sugar and garnish with lemon zest.

NUTRITION PER SERVE

Fat 27.5 g; Protein 6 g; Carbohydrate 51.5 g; Dietary Fibre 1 g; Cholesterol 167 mg; 1960 kJ (470 cal)

COOK'S FILE

Storage: This will keep for 4 days wrapped in foil.

1

2

SOUR CHERRY CAKE

Preparation time: 10 minutes
Total cooking time: 50 minutes
Serves 8–10

125 g unsalted butter, softened
3/4 cup (185 g) caster sugar
2 eggs, lightly beaten
1/2 cup (95 g) ground almonds
1 cup (125 g) self-raising flour
1/2 cup (60 g) plain flour
1/2 cup (125 ml) milk
680 g jar pitted morello cherries, well drained

1 Preheat the oven to moderate 180°C (350°F/Gas 4). Grease and flour a 23 cm fluted baba tin, shaking out the excess flour. Beat the butter and sugar with electric beaters until pale but not creamy. Add the egg gradually, beating well after each addition.

2 Stir in the ground almonds, then fold in the sifted flours alternately with the milk. Gently fold in the cherries. Spoon the mixture into the prepared tin and smooth the surface. Bake for 50 minutes, or until a skewer comes out clean when inserted into the centre of the cake. Leave to cool in the tin for 10 minutes before turning out onto a wire rack to cool. If desired, dust with icing sugar before serving.

NUTRITION PER SERVE (10)
Fat 17.5 g; Protein 6 g; Carbohydrate 40.5 g; Dietary Fibre 2.5 g; Cholesterol 69.5 mg; 1405 kJ (335 cal)

COOK'S FILE
Note: This cake is best eaten on the day it is made.

1

2

CHOCOLATE BANANA CAKE

Preparation time: 15 minutes
Total cooking time: 55 minutes
Serves 6–8

3 ripe bananas, mashed (about 1 cup)
3/4 cup (185 g) caster sugar
1 1/2 cups (185 g) self-raising flour
2 eggs, lightly beaten
3 tablespoons light olive oil
1/4 cup (60 ml) milk
100 g dark chocolate, grated
90 g walnuts, chopped

1 Preheat the oven to moderate 180°C (350°F/Gas 4). Grease a 20 x 10 cm loaf tin and line the base with baking paper. Mix the mashed banana and sugar in a large bowl until just combined.
2 Add the sifted flour, eggs, oil and milk. Stir the mixture gently for 30 seconds with a wooden spoon. Fold in the chocolate and walnuts.
3 Pour the mixture into the tin and bake for 55 minutes, or until a skewer comes out clean when inserted into the centre of the cake. Cool in the tin for 5 minutes before turning onto a wire rack. If desired, serve warm with cream.

NUTRITION PER SERVE (8)
Fat 20.5 g; Protein 7 g; Carbohydrate 58.5 g; Dietary Fibre 3 g; Cholesterol 46 mg; 1830 kJ (435 cal)

COOK'S FILE
Note: In warm weather, chocolate can be grated more easily if placed in the freezer for a few minutes before grating.

1

2

3

CHOCOLATE GINGER AND FIG CAKE

Preparation time: 15 minutes
Total cooking time: 1 hour
Serves 8

125 g unsalted butter, softened
1 cup (230 g) firmly packed soft brown sugar
2 eggs, lightly beaten
1 1/2 cups (185) self-raising flour
1/3 cup (40 g) cocoa powder
3/4 cup (185 ml) milk
2/3 cup (125 g) dried figs, chopped
1/3 cup (75 g) glacé ginger, chopped

1 Preheat the oven to moderate 180°C (350°F/Gas 4). Grease a 22 x 12 cm loaf tin and line the base with baking paper. Beat the butter and sugar with electric beaters until pale and creamy.

2 Gradually add the egg, beating well after each addition. Stir in the sifted flour and cocoa alternately with the milk to make a smooth batter. Fold in the figs and half the ginger.

3 Spoon the mixture into the prepared tin and smooth the surface. Scatter the remaining ginger over the top. Bake for 1 hour, or until a skewer comes out clean when inserted into the centre of the cake. Leave the cake to cool in the tin for 5 minutes before inverting onto a wire rack.

NUTRITION PER SERVE
Fat 16 g; Protein 6.5 g; Carbohydrate 63 g; Dietary Fibre 3.5 g; Cholesterol 88 mg; 1725 kJ (410 cal)

1

2

3

HAZELNUT CREAM SQUARES

Preparation time: 15 minutes
Total cooking time: 25 minutes
Makes 16

4 eggs, separated
1/2 cup (125 g) caster sugar
1/2 cup (60 g) self-raising flour
2/3 cup (75 g) ground hazelnuts
150 g unsalted butter, softened
1/2 cup (170 g) chocolate hazelnut spread
1/2 cup (60 g) icing sugar, sifted
cocoa powder, to dust

1 Preheat the oven to moderate 180°C (350°F/Gas 4). Grease a 20 cm shallow square cake tin and line the base with baking paper. Beat the egg whites with electric beaters in a bowl until soft peaks form. Gradually add the sugar, beating until thick and glossy. Beat the egg yolks into the mixture, one at a time.

2 Sift the flour over the mixture, add the ground hazelnuts and fold in with a metal spoon. Melt 20 g of the butter with 2 tablespoons boiling water in a small bowl, then fold into the sponge mixture. Pour the mixture into the prepared tin and bake for 25 minutes, or until cooked. Leave in the tin for 5 minutes before turning out onto a wire rack to cool. Cut the sponge in half horizontally through the centre.

3 Beat the hazelnut spread and the remaining butter with electric beaters until very creamy. Beat in the icing sugar, then gradually add 3 teaspoons of boiling water and beat until smooth. Fill the cake with the icing mixture and refrigerate until the filling is firm. Dust with the cocoa powder then cut into squares.

NUTRITION PER SQUARE
Fat 15.5 g; Protein 3.5 g; Carbohydrate 21 g; Dietary Fibre 0.8 g; Cholesterol 69.5 mg; 955 kJ (227.5 cal)

1

2

3

ZESTY OLIVE OIL CAKE

Preparation time: 10 minutes
Total cooking time: 45 minutes
Serves 8

2 eggs
2/3 cup (160 g) caster sugar
2 teaspoons finely grated orange rind
2 teaspoons finely grated lemon rind
1/2 cup (125 ml) olive oil
1 1/2 cups (185 g) self-raising flour
1/4 cup (60 ml) milk
1/4 cup (60 ml) orange juice

1 Preheat the oven to moderate 180°C (350°F/Gas 4). Grease a shallow 20 cm round cake tin and line the base with baking paper. Whisk the eggs and sugar in a large bowl until well combined. Add the orange and lemon rind, then stir in the olive oil.

2 Stir in the sifted flour alternately with the milk and orange juice. Stir the mixture gently for 30 seconds with a wooden spoon. Pour into the prepared tin. Bake for 45 minutes, or until a skewer comes out clean when inserted into the centre of the cake. Leave to cool in the tin for 5 minutes before turning out onto a wire rack.

NUTRITION PER SERVE
Fat 16.5 g; Protein 4 g; Carbohydrate 37.5 g; Dietary Fibre 1 g; Cholesterol 46 mg; 1300 kJ (310 cal)

COOK'S FILE
Note: This cake can be dusted with icing sugar before serving, if desired.

1

2

COCONUT, GINGER AND LIME CAKE

Preparation time: 10 minutes
Total cooking time: 50 minutes
Serves 8–10

- 150 g unsalted butter, softened
- 3/4 cup (185 g) caster sugar
- 2 teaspoons grated lime rind
- 2 eggs, lightly beaten
- 1/4 cup (55 g) finely chopped glacé ginger
- 13/4 cups (215 g) self-raising flour
- 1/2 cup (45 g) desiccated coconut
- 3/4 cup (185 ml) milk

1 Preheat the oven to moderate 180°C (350°F/Gas 4). Grease a 22 x 12 cm loaf tin and line the base with baking paper. Beat the butter, sugar and lime rind in a bowl with electric beaters until pale and creamy.

2 Add the egg gradually, beating well between each addition, then add the ginger. Fold in the sifted flour and the coconut alternately with the milk. Spoon the mixture into the prepared tin and smooth the surface. Bake for 50 minutes, or until a skewer comes out clean when inserted into the centre of the cake. Leave in the tin for 5 minutes then turn onto a wire rack to cool. If desired, garnish with lime slices and lime zest and serve with ice cream.

NUTRITION PER SERVE (10)
Fat 17 g; Protein 4.5 g; Carbohydrate 39.5 g; Dietary Fibre 1.5 g; Cholesterol 77 mg; 1355 kJ (325 cal)

1

2

PINEAPPLE PECAN CAKE

Preparation time: 15 minutes
Total cooking time: 1 hour
Serves 8–10

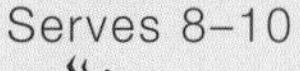

80 g unsalted butter, softened
1 cup (250 g) sugar
2 eggs, lightly beaten
1 1/2 cups (185 g) plain flour
1 3/4 teaspoons baking powder
1/3 cup (40 g) finely chopped pecans, toasted
2/3 cup (180 g) finely chopped glacé pineapple (see Note)
2/3 cup (170 ml) milk

1 Preheat the oven to moderate 180°C (350°F/Gas 4). Grease a 23 cm round cake tin and line the base with baking paper. Beat the butter and sugar with electric beaters until combined. Add the egg and beat until pale and creamy.
2 Sift together the flour, baking powder and 1/4 teaspoon salt. Add to the butter mixture with the nuts, pineapple and milk, then beat on low for 1 minute, or until almost smooth.
3 Spoon the mixture evenly into the prepared tin and smooth the surface. Bake for 1 hour, or until a skewer comes out clean when inserted into the centre of the cake. Leave in the tin for 10 minutes before turning onto a wire rack to cool. If desired, dust with icing sugar just before serving.

NUTRITION PER SERVE (10)
Fat 11.5 g; Protein 4.5 g; Carbohydrate 52 g; Dietary Fibre 1 g; Cholesterol 58.5 mg; 1335 kJ (320 cal)

COOK'S FILE
Note: Glacé pineapple is available from health food stores.

1

2

3

PECAN AND ORANGE LOAF CAKE

Preparation time: 15 minutes
Total cooking time: 1 hour
Serves 8–10

- 3/4 cup (185 g) caster sugar
- 140 g unsalted butter, softened
- 2 eggs, lightly beaten
- 3/4 cup (100 g) ground pecans
- 1 tablespoon grated orange rind
- 1 1/2 cups (185 g) self-raising flour
- 1/2 cup (125 ml) milk
- 1 cup (125 g) icing sugar

1 Preheat the oven to moderate 180°C (350°F/Gas 4). Grease a 22 x 12 cm loaf tin and line the base and the two long sides of the tin with baking paper. Beat the sugar and 125 g of the butter with electric beaters until pale and creamy. Gradually add the eggs, beating well after each addition. Add the pecans and 3 teaspoons of the orange rind, then gently fold in the sifted flour with a metal spoon alternately with the milk. Spoon the mixture into the prepared tin and smooth the surface. Bake for 50–60 minutes, or until a skewer comes out clean when inserted into the centre of the cake. Leave in the tin for 10 minutes before turning onto a wire rack to cool.

2 To make the icing, place the icing sugar, the remaining orange rind and 1–2 tablespoons hot water in a bowl and mix until smooth and combined. Spread the icing over the cooled cake with a flat-bladed knife.

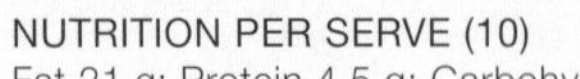

NUTRITION PER SERVE (10)
Fat 21 g; Protein 4.5 g; Carbohydrate 50 g; Dietary Fibre 1.5 g; Cholesterol 73 mg; 1645 kJ (395 cal)

1

2

BEER CAKE

Preparation time: 15 minutes
Total cooking time: 1 hour 50 minutes
Serves 12

- 1 cup (125 g) plain flour
- 1/2 teaspoon ground cinnamon
- 3 cups (750 g) caster sugar
- 275 g unsalted butter, chopped
- 3 eggs
- 4 cups (500 g) self-raising flour
- 3/4 cup (120 g) sultanas
- 2 cups (500 ml) beer

1 Preheat the oven to moderate 180°C (350°F/Gas 4). Grease a deep 25 cm round cake tin and line the base with baking paper. To make the topping, mix together the plain flour, cinnamon and 1 cup (250 g) of the sugar. Place in a food processor with 125 g of the butter and combine.

2 Place the remaining butter in a large bowl with the remaining sugar and beat with electric beaters until pale and creamy. Gradually add the eggs, beating well after each addition—the mixture may look curdled but once you add the flour, it will bring it back together. Fold in the sifted flour, sultanas and beer.

3 Pour the mixture into the prepared tin and clump the topping together in your hands to form small balls, then sprinkle over the cake. Bake for 1 hour 50 minutes, or until a skewer comes out clean when inserted into the centre. Leave to cool in the tin before inverting onto a wire rack. If desired, serve with cream.

NUTRITION PER SERVE
Fat 21 g; Protein 7.5 g; Carbohydrate 108 g; Dietary Fibre 2.5 g; Cholesterol 103.5 mg; 2705 kJ (645 cal)

1

2

3

INDIVIDUAL WHITE CHOCOLATE CHIP CAKES

Preparation time: 15 minutes
Total cooking time: 20 minutes
Makes 12

125 g unsalted butter, softened
3/4 cup (185 g) caster sugar
2 eggs, lightly beaten
1 teaspoon vanilla essence
2 cups (250 g) self-raising flour, sifted
1/2 cup (125 ml) buttermilk
1 1/4 cups (280 g) white chocolate chips

1 Preheat the oven to warm 170°C (325°F/Gas 3). Lightly grease twelve 1/2 cup (125 ml) muffin tins.
2 Beat the butter and sugar in a large bowl with electric beaters until pale and creamy. Gradually add the egg, beating well after each addition. Add the vanilla essence and beat until combined. Fold in the flour alternately with the buttermilk, then fold in the chocolate chips.
3 Fill each muffin hole three-quarters full with the mixture and bake for 20 minutes, or until a skewer comes out clean when inserted into the centre of each cake. Leave in the tin for 5 minutes before turning out onto a wire rack to cool—loosen around the edges if the cakes stick to the tin.

NUTRITION PER CAKE
Fat 17.5 g; Protein 5 g; Carbohydrate 43.5 g; Dietary Fibre 1 g; Cholesterol 62 mg; 1460 kJ (350 cal)

COOK'S FILE
Note: Top with White chocolate cream cheese icing (see page 6) and garnish with white chocolate shavings.

1

2

3

BUTTERFLY CUPCAKES

Preparation time: 10 minutes
Total cooking time: 30 minutes
Makes 12

120 g unsalted butter, softened
2/3 cup (180 g) caster sugar
1 1/2 cups (185 g) self-raising flour
1/2 cup (125 ml) milk
2 eggs
1/2 cup (125 ml) thick cream
1/4 cup (40 g) strawberry jam
icing sugar, to dust

1 Preheat the oven to moderate 180°C (350°F/Gas 4). Line a flat-bottomed 12-hole cupcake tray with paper patty cases. Beat the butter, sugar, flour, milk and eggs with electric beaters on low speed. Increase the speed and beat until smooth and pale. Divide evenly among the cases and bake for 30 minutes, or until cooked and golden. Transfer to a wire rack to cool.

2 Cut shallow rounds from the centre of each cake using the point of a sharp knife, then cut in half. Spoon 2 teaspoons cream into each cavity, top with 1 teaspoon jam and position two halves of the cake tops in the jam to resemble butterfly wings. Dust with icing sugar.

NUTRITION PER CUPCAKE
Fat 13.5 g; Protein 3 g; Carbohydrate 29 g; Dietary Fibre 0.5 g; Cholesterol 69 mg; 1025 kJ (245 cal)

COOK'S FILE
Note: If using foil patty cases instead of the standard paper cases as suggested, the size and number of butterfly cakes may vary.

1

2

DEVIL'S FOOD CAKE

Preparation time: 15 minutes
Total cooking time: 50 minutes
Serves 8

1 1/3 cups (165 g) plain flour
2/3 cup (85 g) cocoa powder
1 teaspoon bicarbonate of soda
1 cup (250 g) sugar
1 cup (250 ml) buttermilk
2 eggs, lightly beaten
125 g unsalted butter, softened
1/2 cup (125 ml) cream, whipped

1 Preheat the oven to moderate 180°C (350°F/Gas 4). Grease a deep 20 cm round cake tin and line the base with baking paper. Sift the flour, cocoa and bicarbonate of soda into a large bowl.

2 Add the sugar to the sifted dry ingredients. Combine the buttermilk, eggs and butter, then pour onto the dry ingredients. Beat with electric beaters on low speed for 3 minutes, or until just combined. Increase the speed to high and beat for 3 minutes, or until the mixture is free of lumps and increased in volume.

3 Spoon the mixture into the prepared tin and smooth the surface. Bake for 40–50 minutes, or until a skewer comes out clean when inserted into the centre of the cake. Leave in the tin for 15 minutes before turning out onto a wire rack to cool completely. Cut the cake in half horizontally and fill with the whipped cream. If desired, dust with icing sugar and garnish with fresh berries.

NUTRITION PER SERVE
Fat 23 g; Protein 7.5 g; Carbohydrate 52 g; Dietary Fibre 1.5 g; Cholesterol 109 mg; 1840 kJ (440 cal)

COOK'S FILE
Storage: Unfilled, the cake will keep for 3 days in an airtight container or up to 3 months in the freezer. The filled cake is best assembled and eaten on the day of baking.

1

2

3

PUMPKIN FRUITCAKE

Preparation time: 15 minutes
Total cooking time: 1 hour 50 minutes
Serves 8–10

- 250 g pumpkin, peeled and cut into small pieces
- 125 g unsalted butter, softened
- 3/4 cup (140 g) lightly packed soft brown sugar
- 2 tablespoons golden syrup
- 2 eggs, lightly beaten
- 2 cups (250 g) self-raising flour, sifted
- 200 g mixed dried fruit
- 2 tablespoons chopped glacé ginger

1 Preheat the oven to slow 150°C (300°F/Gas 2). Grease a deep 20 cm round cake tin and line the base and side with baking paper. Steam the pumpkin for 10 minutes, or until cooked through. Mash with a potato masher or a fork until smooth. Measure 3/4 cup (200 g) and set aside until ready to use.

2 Beat the butter and sugar together with electric beaters until pale and creamy. Add the golden syrup and beat well. Gradually add the egg, beating well after each addition. Fold in the pumpkin until combined. Combine the flour, dried fruit and ginger, then fold into the butter mixture with a metal spoon until combined.

3 Spoon the mixture into the prepared tin and smooth the surface. Bake for 1 hour 40 minutes, or until a skewer comes out clean when inserted into the centre of the cake. Cool in the tin for 20 minutes before turning out onto a wire rack.

NUTRITION PER SERVE (10)
Fat 12 g; Protein 4.5 g; Carbohydrate 52 g; Dietary Fibre 2.5 g; Cholesterol 67.5 mg; 1375 kJ (330 cal)

1

2

3

CARROT, SPICE AND SOUR CREAM CAKE

Preparation time: 15 minutes
Total cooking time: 1 hour 15 minutes
Serves 8–10

2 1/2 cups (310 g) self-raising flour
2 teaspoons ground cinnamon
1 teaspoon ground nutmeg
1 cup (150 g) dark brown sugar
2 cups (200 g) grated carrot (about 260 g carrots)
4 eggs
1 cup (250 g) sour cream
1 cup (250 ml) vegetable oil

1 Preheat the oven to warm 160°C (315°F/Gas 2–3). Grease a deep 22 cm round tin and line the base with baking paper. Sift the flour and spices into a large bowl, then stir in the brown sugar and grated carrot until well mixed.

2 Combine the eggs, sour cream and oil until lightly beaten. Add to the carrot mixture and stir until well combined. Spoon the mixture into the prepared tin and smooth the surface. Bake for 1 hour 15 minutes, or until a skewer comes out clean when inserted into the centre of the cake. Leave in the tin for 10 minutes before turning out onto a wire rack to cool completely.

NUTRITION PER SERVE (10)
Fat 35.5 g; Protein 7 g; Carbohydrate 38.5 g; Dietary Fibre 2 g; Cholesterol 104.5 mg; 2055 kJ (490 cal)

COOK'S FILE
Note: Ice with Orange cream cheese frosting (see page 6).

1

2

APRICOT AND RAISIN BRAN LOAF

Preparation time: 15 minutes + 30 minutes soaking
Total cooking time: 50 minutes
Serves 6–8

150 g dried apricots, chopped
1 cup (160 g) raisins
1 cup (70 g) processed bran cereal
1/2 cup (95 g) lightly packed soft brown sugar
1 1/2 cups (375 ml) warm milk
1 cup (125 g) self-raising flour, sifted
1/2 cup (75 g) wholemeal self-raising flour, sifted
1 teaspoon mixed spice

1 Preheat the oven to moderate 180°C (350°F/Gas 4). Grease a deep 18.5 x 11 cm loaf tin and line the base and sides with baking paper. Soak the apricots, raisins, bran cereal and brown sugar in the milk in a large bowl for 30 minutes, or until the milk is almost completely absorbed. Stir in the flours and mixed spice to form a stiff moist batter.

2 Spoon the mixture into the prepared tin and smooth the surface. Bake for 50 minutes, or until a skewer comes out clean when inserted into the centre of the cake—cover with foil during cooking if it browns too much. Leave in the tin for 10 minutes before turning out onto a wire rack to cool. Cut into thick slices. If desired, serve with butter and dust with icing sugar.

NUTRITION PER SERVE (8)
Fat 3 g; Protein 6.5 g; Carbohydrate 52.5 g; Dietary Fibre 7 g; Cholesterol 6.5 mg; 1085 kJ (260 cal)

COOK'S FILE
Note: Use any dried fruit combination. This loaf is delicious toasted.

1

2

WALNUT CAKE WITH CHOCOLATE ICING

Preparation time: 15 minutes
Total cooking time: 40 minutes
Serves 6

185 g unsalted butter, softened
1/2 cup (95 g) lightly packed soft brown sugar
2 eggs
1 1/2 cups (185 g) self-raising flour
3/4 cup (90 g) chopped walnuts
1/4 cup (60 ml) milk

Chocolate icing
125 g good-quality dark chocolate, chopped
20 g unsalted butter

1 Preheat the oven to moderate 180°C (350°F/Gas 4). Grease a 20 cm springform tin and line the base with baking paper. Place the butter and sugar in a large bowl. Beat with electric beaters for 5 minutes, or until thick and creamy. Add the eggs one at a time, beating well after each addition. Fold in the flour and 1/2 cup (60 g) of the walnuts alternately with the milk until just combined. Spoon the mixture into the prepared tin and smooth the surface. Bake for 35 minutes, or until a skewer comes out clean when inserted into the centre of the cake. Leave in the tin for 5 minutes before turning out onto a wire rack to cool.

2 To make the icing, place the chocolate and butter in a heatproof bowl. Bring a saucepan of water to the boil, then reduce the heat to a gentle simmer. Sit the bowl over the saucepan, making sure the base of the bowl does not touch the water. Stir occasionally to ensure even melting. Cool slightly, then spread over the cake. Sprinkle with the remaining walnuts.

NUTRITION PER SERVE
Fat 47 g; Protein 9 g; Carbohydrate 51.5 g; Dietary Fibre 2.5 g; Cholesterol 147.5 mg; 2735 kJ (655 cal)

1

2

LEMON SEMOLINA CAKE

Preparation time: 15 minutes
Total cooking time: 45 minutes
Serves 8–10

6 eggs, separated
1 1/4 cups (310 g) caster sugar
2 teaspoons finely grated lemon rind
1/3 cup (80 ml) lemon juice
3/4 cup (90 g) semolina
1/2 cup (95 g) ground almonds
2 tablespoons self-raising flour
thick cream, to serve

1 Preheat the oven to warm 170°C (325°F/Gas 3). Grease a 24 cm springform tin and line the base with baking paper. Place the yolks, 1 cup (250 g) of the sugar, the lemon rind and 2 tablespoons of the lemon juice in a large bowl. Beat with electric beaters for 8 minutes, or until thick and pale and the mixture leaves a trail when the beaters are lifted.

2 Beat the egg whites in a clean bowl with clean electric beaters until firm peaks form. Gently fold the whites into the egg yolk mixture alternately with the combined semolina, ground almonds and flour. Take care not to overmix or the mixture will deflate. Carefully pour into the prepared tin and smooth the surface. Bake for 35–40 minutes, or until a skewer comes out clean when inserted into the centre of the cake. Leave for 5 minutes in the tin then turn out onto a wire rack to cool. Pierce a few holes in the cake with a skewer.

3 Place the remaining lemon juice and sugar in a small saucepan with 1/2 cup (125 ml) water. Stir over low heat until the sugar has dissolved. Increase the heat and simmer for 3 minutes, or until thick and syrupy. Pour the hot syrup over the cooled cake. Serve with thick cream.

NUTRITION PER SERVE (10)
Fat 6 g; Protein 6 g; Carbohydrate 39 g; Dietary Fibre 1 g; Cholesterol 108 mg; 955 kJ (230 cal)

1

2

3

CHOCOLATE, ALMOND AND MIXED PEEL CAKE

Preparation time: 15 minutes
Total cooking time: 45 minutes
Serves 6

1 tablespoon mixed peel, chopped
150 g dark chocolate pieces
1/2 cup (95 g) ground almonds
1/2 cup (60 g) self-raising flour
4 eggs, separated
1/2 cup (125 g) caster sugar
2 tablespoons warm milk
2/3 cup (170 ml) cream, whipped

1 Preheat the oven to moderate 180°C (350°F/Gas 4). Grease a 20 cm springform tin and line the base with baking paper. Combine the mixed peel and 100 g of the chocolate in a food processor until finely ground. Add the ground almonds and flour and process briefly to combine.

2 Beat the egg yolks and sugar with electric beaters for 5 minutes, or until thick and pale—the beaters should leave a trail in the mixture. Stir in the chocolate and peel mixture, then the milk. Beat the egg whites in a clean bowl until soft peaks form. Gently fold the whites into the cake mixture with a metal spoon—do not overmix, or it will lose volume. Pour the mixture into the prepared tin and smooth the surface. Bake for 45 minutes, or until a skewer comes out clean when inserted into the centre of the cake. Leave in the tin for 5 minutes then turn out onto a wire rack to cool.

3 To make the filling, melt the remaining chocolate pieces in a small heatproof bowl over a saucepan of hot water. Cut the cake in half horizontally through the centre. Spread the bottom layer with melted chocolate, then the whipped cream. Cover with the remaining layer and, if desired, dust with icing sugar in a pattern.

NUTRITION PER SERVE
Fat 28 g; Protein 9.5 g; Carbohydrate 49 g; Dietary Fibre 1.5 g; Cholesterol 159.5 mg; 1990 kJ (475 cal)

1

2

3

SAND CAKE

Preparation time: 10 minutes
Total cooking time: 50 minutes
Serves 8–10

185 g unsalted butter, softened
2 teaspoons vanilla essence
1 cup (250 g) caster sugar
3 eggs
1 1/2 cups (185 g) self-raising flour
1/3 cup (60 g) rice flour
1/3 cup (80 ml) milk

1 Preheat the oven to moderate 180°C (350°F/Gas 4). Grease a 23 cm square tin and line the base with baking paper.
2 Beat the butter, vanilla, sugar, eggs, flours and milk with electric beaters until combined, then beat at medium speed for 3 minutes, or until thick and creamy.
3 Pour the mixture into the prepared tin and smooth the surface. Bake for 50 minutes, or until a skewer comes out clean when inserted into the centre of the cake. Leave for 10 minutes in the tin then turn out onto a wire rack to cool.

NUTRITION PER SERVE (10)
Fat 17 g; Protein 4.5 g; Carbohydrate 43.5 g; Dietary Fibre 1 g; Cholesterol 102.5 mg; 1435 kJ (345 cal)

COOK'S FILE
Note: Cover with Passionfruit icing (see page 7). Rose buds make a lovely garnish, but make sure you remove them before eating the cake.

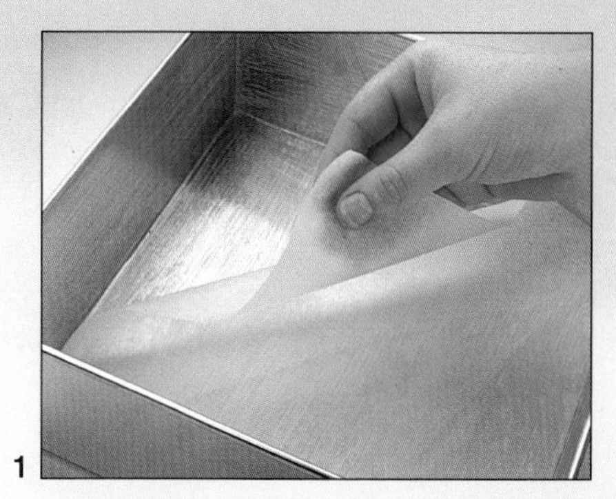
1

2

3

ORANGE POPPY SEED CAKE WITH CITRUS ICING

Preparation time: 15 minutes + 15 minutes soaking
Total cooking time: 50 minutes
Serves 8

- 1/3 cup (50 g) poppy seeds
- 3/4 cup (185 ml) warm milk
- 1 cup (250 g) caster sugar
- 3 eggs
- 2 cups (250 g) self-raising flour, sifted
- 210 g unsalted butter, softened

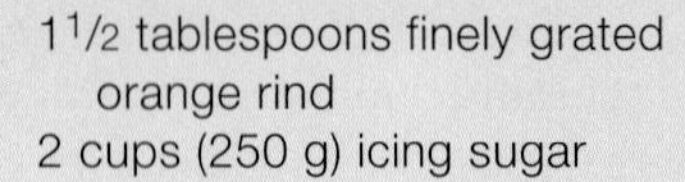

- 1 1/2 tablespoons finely grated orange rind
- 2 cups (250 g) icing sugar

1 Preheat the oven to moderate 180°C (350°F/Gas 4). Lightly grease a 23 cm fluted baba tin. Combine the poppy seeds and milk in a bowl and set aside for at least 15 minutes.

2 Place the caster sugar, eggs, flour, 185 g of the butter and 3 teaspoons of the orange rind in a large bowl. Add the poppy seed mixture and beat with electric beaters on low speed until combined. Increase to medium speed and beat for 3 minutes, or until the mixture is thick and pale. Pour the mixture evenly into the prepared tin. Bake for 50 minutes, or until a skewer comes out clean when inserted into the centre of the cake. Leave in the tin for 5 minutes then turn out onto a wire rack.

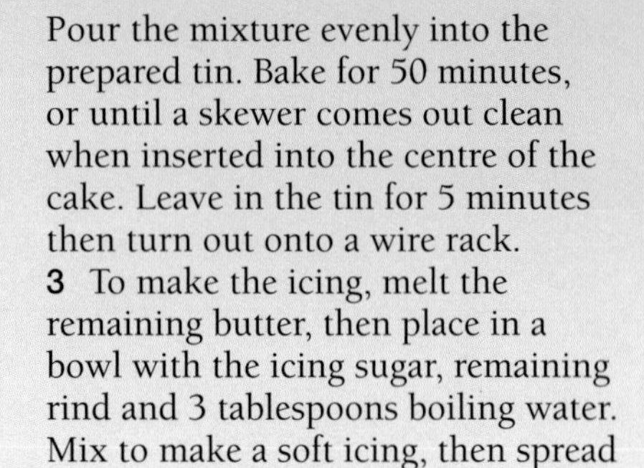

3 To make the icing, melt the remaining butter, then place in a bowl with the icing sugar, remaining rind and 3 tablespoons boiling water. Mix to make a soft icing, then spread over the warm cake.

NUTRITION PER SERVE

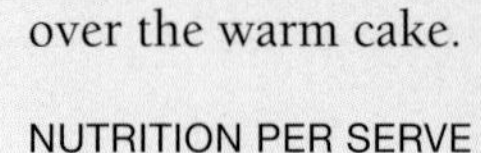

Fat 27.5 g; Protein 7.5 g; Carbohydrate 93 g; Dietary Fibre 2.5 g; Cholesterol 138 mg; 2650 kJ (635 cal)

1

2

3

SPONGE SANDWICH WITH JAM AND CREAM

Preparation time: 15 minutes
Total cooking time: 20 minutes
Serves 8

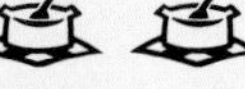

4 eggs
1 teaspoon vanilla essence
1/2 cup (125 g) caster sugar
1/2 cup (60 g) self-raising flour
1/2 cup (60 g) cornflour
2 tablespoons raspberry jam
300 ml cream, whipped
icing sugar, to dust

1 Preheat the oven to moderate 180°C (350°F/Gas 4). Grease two shallow 20 cm sponge tins and line each base with baking paper. Beat the eggs, vanilla and sugar with electric beaters for 5 minutes, or until pale and creamy—the beaters should leave a trail in the mixture.

2 Sift the flours together on a sheet of baking paper. Gently tip the flour into the egg and sugar mixture and fold quickly and lightly using a large metal spoon—do not overmix or it will lose volume. Divide the mixture evenly between the tins. Bake for 20 minutes, or until a skewer comes out clean when inserted into the centre of each cake. Leave in the tins for 5 minutes then turn out onto a wire rack to cool completely. Spread one cake with the jam and cream, then place the other cake on top. Dust with icing sugar to serve, and if desired, decorate with coloured cachous.

NUTRITION PER SERVE
Fat 18.5 g; Protein 4.5 g; Carbohydrate 33 g; Dietary Fibre 0.5 g; Cholesterol 141 mg; 1300 kJ (310 cal)

1

2

BANANA SOUR CREAM CAKE

Preparation time: 15 minutes
Total cooking time: 1 hour 45 minutes
Serves 8–10

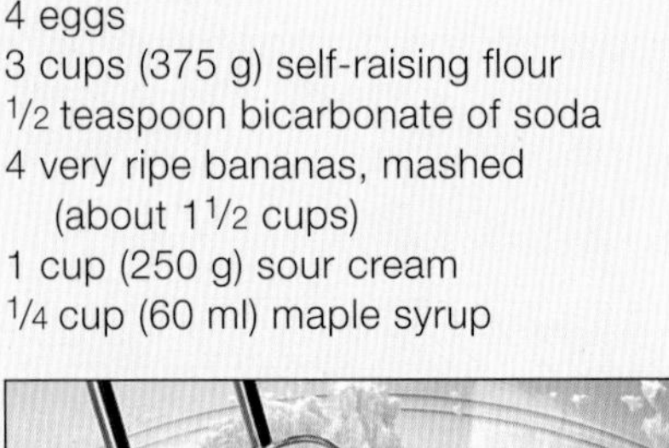

250 g unsalted butter, softened
1 3/4 cups (435 g) sugar
4 eggs
3 cups (375 g) self-raising flour
1/2 teaspoon bicarbonate of soda
4 very ripe bananas, mashed (about 1 1/2 cups)
1 cup (250 g) sour cream
1/4 cup (60 ml) maple syrup

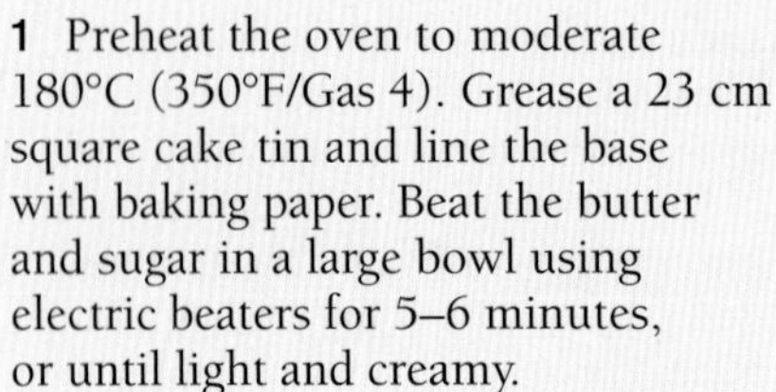

1 Preheat the oven to moderate 180°C (350°F/Gas 4). Grease a 23 cm square cake tin and line the base with baking paper. Beat the butter and sugar in a large bowl using electric beaters for 5–6 minutes, or until light and creamy.

2 Add the eggs one at a time, beating well after each addition. Sift the flour and bicarbonate of soda together, then fold in alternately with the mashed banana and the combined sour cream and maple syrup until well combined.

3 Spoon the mixture into the tin and smooth the surface. Bake for 1 hour 45 minutes, or until a skewer comes out clean when inserted into the centre of the cake. Leave in the tin for 5 minutes then turn out onto a wire rack to cool.

NUTRITION PER SERVE (10)
Fat 32 g; Protein 8 g; Carbohydrate 87.5 g; Dietary Fibre 2.5 g; Cholesterol 166 mg; 2745 kJ (655 cal)

COOK'S FILE
Note: Cover with Lemon cream cheese icing (see page 6).

1

2

3

COCONUT SYRUP CAKE

Preparation time: 10 minutes + 2 hours soaking
Total cooking time: 50 minutes
Serves 12

200 g unsalted butter, softened
1 1/2 cups (375 g) caster sugar
6 eggs
1 1/2 cups (185 g) self-raising flour
3 cups (270 g) desiccated coconut

Syrup
1 tablespoon lemon zest
1 1/2 cups (375 g) sugar

1 Preheat the oven to moderate 180°C (350°F/Gas 4). Grease and flour a 2 litre fluted baba tin or tube tin. Shake off the excess flour. Beat the butter and sugar together with electric beaters for 5 minutes, or until pale and creamy. Add the eggs one at a time, beating well after each addition, until combined. Fold in the flour and coconut and mix well.

2 Spoon the mixture into the tin and bake for 45 minutes, or until a skewer comes out clean when inserted into the centre of the cake. Cool slightly in the tin, then turn out onto a wire rack.

3 To make the syrup, place the zest, sugar and 1 cup (250 ml) water in a small saucepan. Stir over medium heat until the sugar has dissolved. Cool to room temperature. Pierce the cake all over with a skewer, pour the syrup over the cake and leave for 2 hours to soak up the syrup. If desired, garnish with shaved coconut.

NUTRITION PER SERVE
Fat 30 g; Protein 6.5 g; Carbohydrate 59.5 g; Dietary Fibre 4 g; Cholesterol 132.5 mg; 2190 kJ (525 cal)

1

2

3

PASSIONFRUIT AND PAWPAW POUND CAKE

Preparation time: 15 minutes
Total cooking time: 1 hour 15 minutes
Serves 16

315 g self-raising flour
1/2 cup (60 g) custard powder
1 1/2 cups (375 g) sugar
1/2 cup (125 ml) milk
3 eggs
200 g unsalted butter, softened
170 ml can passionfruit in syrup
100 g dried pawpaw, diced

1 Preheat the oven to moderate 180°C (350°F/Gas 4). Grease a 23 cm square cake tin and line the base with baking paper. Sift the flour and custard powder into a large bowl.
2 Add the sugar, milk, eggs, butter and passionfruit and beat with electric beaters on medium speed for 10 minutes. Fold in the pawpaw until combined.
3 Pour the mixture into the tin and bake for 1 hour 15 minutes. Leave to cool in the tin for 5 minutes before turning out onto a wire rack. If desired, serve with ice cream, fresh mango and passionfruit.

NUTRITION PER SERVE
Fat 12 g; Protein 4 g; Carbohydrate 45 g; Dietary Fibre 3 g; Cholesterol 67 mg; 1250 kJ (300 cal)

COOK'S FILE
Note: This pound cake is moist and will keep for several days, covered, wrapped in plastic and stored in an airtight container.

1

2

3

CARAMEL PEACH CAKE

Preparation time: 15 minutes + 30 minutes standing
Total cooking time: 1 hour 25 minutes
Serves 10–12

250 g unsalted butter, softened
1/3 cup (60 g) lightly packed soft brown sugar
825 g can peach halves in natural juice
1 cup (250 g) caster sugar
3 teaspoons finely grated lemon rind
3 eggs, lightly beaten
2 1/2 cups (310 g) self-raising flour, sifted
1 cup (250 g) plain yoghurt

1 Preheat the oven to moderate 180°C (350°F/Gas 4). Grease a deep 23 cm round cake tin and line the base with baking paper. Melt 50 g of the butter and pour on the base of the tin. Evenly sprinkle the brown sugar on top. Drain the peaches, reserving 1 tablespoon of the liquid. Arrange the peach halves, cut-side-up, over the sugar mixture.

2 Beat the caster sugar, lemon rind and remaining butter with electric beaters for 5–6 minutes, or until pale and creamy. Add the egg gradually, beating well after each addition—the mixture may look curdled but once you add the flour, it will bring it back together. Using a metal spoon, fold in the flour alternately with the yoghurt (in two batches) then the reserved peach liquid. Spoon the mixture over the peaches in the tin and smooth the surface. Bake for 1 hour 25 minutes, or until a skewer comes out clean when inserted into the centre of the cake. Leave to cool in the tin for 30 minutes before carefully turning out onto a large serving plate.

NUTRITION PER SERVE (12)
Fat 19.5 g; Protein 5.5 g; Carbohydrate 52 g; Dietary Fibre 2 g; Cholesterol 100 mg; 1670 kJ (400 cal)

1

2

RAISIN BUTTER CAKE

Preparation time: 15 minutes
Total cooking time: 1 hour 30 minutes
Serves 10

1 cup (160 g) raisins
1/4 cup (60 ml) rum
1 tablespoon firmly packed soft brown sugar
250 g unsalted butter, softened
1 cup (230 g) firmly packed soft brown sugar, extra
3 eggs, lightly beaten
2 1/2 cups (310 g) self-raising flour, sifted
3/4 cup (185 ml) buttermilk

1 Preheat the oven to moderate 180°C (350°F/Gas 4). Lightly grease a 23 cm round cake tin and line the base with baking paper. Combine the raisins, rum and brown sugar in a small saucepan. Bring to the boil, reduce the heat and simmer for 30 seconds, or until the rum is absorbed. Set aside to cool.
2 Beat the butter and extra brown sugar with electric beaters until pale and creamy. Add the egg gradually, beating well after each addition—the mixture may look curdled but once you add the flour, it will bring it back together. Use a metal spoon to fold in the sifted flour and buttermilk in two batches. Fold in the raisin and rum mixture.
3 Spoon the mixture into the tin and bake for 1 hour 30 minutes, or until a skewer comes out clean when inserted into the centre of the cake. Leave in the tin for 10 minutes before carefully turning onto a wire rack to cool.

NUTRITION PER SERVE
Fat 23 g; Protein 6 g; Carbohydrate 55.5 g; Dietary Fibre 2 g; Cholesterol 120 mg; 1915 kJ (455 cal)

COOK'S FILE
Note: Cover with Coffee buttercream (see page 7). If desired, top with extra raisins or flaked almonds.

1

2

3

APRICOT PINE NUT CAKE

Preparation time: 15 minutes
Total cooking time: 1 hour 30 minutes
Serves 10

2/3 cup (100 g) pine nuts, roughly chopped
250 g unsalted butter, softened
1 cup (250 g) sugar
3 teaspoons finely grated orange rind
3 eggs, lightly beaten
2 1/2 cups (310 g) self-raising flour, sifted
1 cup (200 g) glacé apricots, finely chopped
1 cup (250 ml) orange juice

1 Preheat the oven to moderate 180°C (350°F/Gas 4). Lightly grease a 26 cm round cake tin and line the base with baking paper. Spread the pine nuts on a baking tray and bake for 5–10 minutes, or until lightly golden. Set aside to cool.
2 Beat the butter, sugar and orange rind with electric beaters until pale and creamy. Add the egg gradually, beating well after each addition—the mixture may look curdled but once you add the flour, it will bring it back together. Fold in the sifted flour, pine nuts, apricots and orange juice in two batches with a metal spoon.
3 Spoon the mixture into the prepared tin and smooth the surface. Bake for 1 hour 20 minutes, or until a skewer comes out clean when inserted into the centre of the cake. Leave in the tin for 10 minutes before turning onto a wire rack to cool. If desired, dust with icing sugar and serve with cream or yoghurt.

NUTRITION PER SERVE
Fat 29.5 g; Protein 7 g; Carbohydrate 62.5 g; Dietary Fibre 2 g; Cholesterol 117 mg; 2235 kJ (535 cal)

COOK'S FILE
Note: The chopped apricots may clump together, so flour your hands and rub through to separate.
Variation: For a little extra flavour, add 2 tablespoons brandy to the cake mixture with the flour, pine nuts, apricots and orange juice.

1

2

3

PRUNE AND RICOTTA CAKE

Preparation time: 10 minutes
Total cooking time: 2 hours
Serves 8

2/3 cup (150 g) pitted prunes, chopped
2 tablespoons Marsala
500 g ricotta
1 cup (250 g) caster sugar
3 eggs, lightly beaten
1/2 cup (125 ml) cream
1/2 cup (60 g) cornflour, sifted
1/2 cup (60 g) grated dark chocolate

1 Preheat the oven to warm 160°C (315°F/Gas 2–3). Lightly grease a 23 cm round cake tin and line the base with baking paper. Combine the prunes and Marsala in a small saucepan. Bring to the boil, reduce the heat and simmer for 30 seconds, or until the Marsala is absorbed. Allow to cool.

2 Beat the ricotta and sugar with electric beaters for 4 minutes, or until light and creamy. Gradually add the egg, beating well after each addition. Add the cream and beat for 2 minutes. Fold in the cornflour, prune mixture and chocolate with a metal spoon.

3 Spoon the mixture into the prepared tin and bake for 2 hours, or until firm and a skewer comes out clean when inserted into the centre of the cake. Leave in the tin for 15–20 minutes before gently turning out onto a wire rack to cool.

NUTRITION PER SERVE
Fat 18 g; Protein 10 g; Carbohydrate 53 g; Dietary Fibre 1.5 g; Cholesterol 118.5 mg; 1710 kJ (410 cal)

COOK'S FILE
Note: To make the star pattern, first dust with icing sugar. Place cardboard cut-outs of stars (or other shapes) gently on top, then dust with cocoa powder.

1

2

3

COFFEE CUPCAKES

Preparation time: 15 minutes
Total cooking time: 30 minutes
Makes 24

195 g unsalted butter, softened
2/3 cup (125 g) lightly packed soft brown sugar
2 eggs
1 tablespoon coffee and chicory essence
1 1/4 cups (155 g) self-raising flour
100 ml buttermilk
1 cup (125 g) icing sugar

1 Preheat the oven to slow 150°C (300°F/Gas 2). Line two 50 ml 12-hole cupcake trays with paper patty cases. Beat 185 g of the butter and the brown sugar with electric beaters until light and creamy. Add the eggs one at a time, beating well after each addition. Mix in 3 teaspoons of the coffee and chicory essence.

2 Fold the flour and a pinch of salt alternately with the buttermilk into the creamed mixture until combined. Spoon èvenly into the patty cake cases and bake for 25–30 minutes, or until just springy to the touch. Leave to cool in the tins.

3 To make the icing, combine the remaining butter, remaining essence, the icing sugar and 1 1/2 tablespoons boiling water in a small bowl. Spread a little icing over each cupcake with a pallete knife until evenly covered. If desired, decorate with chocolate-coated coffee beans.

NUTRITION PER CUPCAKE
Fat 7.5 g; Protein 1.5 g; Carbohydrate 16 g; Dietary Fibre 0.5 g; Cholesterol 36 mg; 550 kJ (130 cal)

1

2

3

ANGEL FOOD CAKE WITH CHOCOLATE SAUCE

Preparation time: 15 minutes
Total cooking time: 45 minutes
Serves 8

1 cup (125 g) plain flour
1 cup (250 g) caster sugar
10 egg whites, at room temperature
1 teaspoon cream of tartar
1/2 teaspoon vanilla essence

Chocolate sauce
250 g dark chocolate, chopped
3/4 cup (185 ml) cream
50 g unsalted butter, chopped

1 Preheat the oven to moderate 180°C (350°F/Gas 4). Have an ungreased angel cake tin ready. Sift the flour and 1/2 cup (125 g) of the sugar four times into a large bowl. Set aside. Beat the egg whites, cream of tartar and 1/4 teaspoon salt in a clean large bowl with electric beaters until soft peaks form. Gradually add the remaining sugar and beat until thick and glossy.

2 Add the vanilla essence. Sift half the flour and sugar mixture over the meringue and gently fold into the mixture with a metal spoon. Repeat with the remaining flour and sugar. Spoon into the cake tin and bake for 45 minutes, or until a skewer comes out clean when inserted into the centre of the cake. Gently loosen around the side of the cake with a spatula, then turn the cake out onto a wire rack to cool completely.

3 To make the sauce, place the chocolate, cream and butter in a saucepan. Stir over low heat until the chocolate has melted and the mixture is smooth. Drizzle over the cake and serve.

NUTRITION PER SERVE
Fat 24 g; Protein 8 g; Carbohydrate 63 g; Dietary Fibre 1 g; Cholesterol 47.5 mg; 2055 kJ (490 cal)

COOK'S FILE
Note: Ensure the tin is very clean and not greased or the cake will not rise and will slip down the side of the tin.

1

2

3

MINI MANGO CAKES WITH LIME SYRUP

Preparation time: 15 minutes
Total cooking time: 35 minutes
Makes 4

425 g can mango slices in syrup, drained
90 g unsalted butter, softened
3/4 cup (185 g) caster sugar
2 eggs, lightly beaten
1/2 cup (60 g) self-raising flour
2 tablespoons ground almonds
2 tablespoons coconut milk
2 tablespoons lime juice

1 Preheat the oven to moderately hot 200°C (400°F/Gas 6). Grease four 1 cup (250 ml) muffin holes and line with mango slices. Beat the butter and 1/2 cup (125 g) of the sugar in a bowl with electric beaters until light and creamy. Gradually add the egg, beating well after each addition. Fold in the sifted flour, then add the almonds and coconut milk, then spoon into the muffin holes. Bake for 25 minutes, or until a skewer comes out clean when inserted into the centre of the cakes.

2 To make the syrup, place the lime juice, the remaining sugar and 1/2 cup (125 ml) water in a small saucepan and stir over low heat until the sugar dissolves. Increase the heat and simmer for 10 minutes. Pierce holes in each cake with a skewer. Drizzle the syrup over the top and allow to stand for 5 minutes to soak up the liquid. Turn out and serve.

NUTRITION PER CAKE
Fat 25.5 g; Protein 7 g; Carbohydrate 64 g; Dietary Fibre 2 g; Cholesterol 147.5 mg; 2100 kJ (500 cal)

1

2

RICH BUTTER CAKE

Preparation time: 10 minutes
Total cooking time: 1 hour 10 minutes
Serves 6–8

250 g unsalted butter, softened
1 cup (250 g) caster sugar
4 eggs
1 teaspoon vanilla essence
1 1/2 cups (185 g) self-raising flour
1/2 cup (60 g) plain flour
3/4 cup (185 ml) milk
icing sugar, to dust

1 Preheat the oven to moderate 180°C (350°F/Gas 4). Lightly grease a deep 20 cm round cake tin and line the base with baking paper. Beat the butter and sugar with electric beaters until light and creamy. Add the eggs one at a time, beating well after each addition.

2 Add the vanilla essence and beat until combined. Sift the flours together and fold in alternately with the milk. Stir until the ingredients are just combined and the mixture is almost smooth. Spoon the mixture into the tin and smooth the surface. Bake for 1 hour 10 minutes, or until a skewer comes out clean when inserted into the centre of the cake. Leave in the tin for 10 minutes before turning onto a wire rack to cool. Dust with the icing sugar and, if desired, serve with fresh raspberries and cream.

NUTRITION PER SERVE (8)
Fat 29.5 g; Protein 7 g; Carbohydrate 54.5 g; Dietary Fibre 1 g; Cholesterol 173 mg; 2105 kJ (500 cal)

1

2

APPLE TEACAKE

Preparation time: 15 minutes
Total cooking time: 1 hour
Serves 8

150 g unsalted butter, chopped
200 g caster sugar
2 eggs, lightly beaten
1 teaspoon vanilla essence
1 1/2 cups (185 g) self-raising flour, sifted
2/3 cup (185 g) vanilla-flavoured yoghurt
1 apple (Granny Smith), peeled, cored and thinly sliced
1 teaspoon ground cinnamon

1 Preheat the oven to moderate 180°C (350°F/Gas 4). Grease a deep 20 cm round cake tin and line the base with baking paper. Beat 130 g of the butter and 3/4 cup (185 g) of the sugar with electric beaters until light and creamy.

2 Gradually add the egg, beating well after each addition until combined. Add the vanilla essence. Fold in the flour, then the yoghurt and stir until smooth. Spoon the mixture into the prepared tin and smooth the surface.

3 Arrange the apple slices evenly over the mixture in a circular pattern starting in the centre. Sprinkle with the cinnamon and the remaining sugar. Melt the remaining butter, then drizzle over the top. Bake for 1 hour, or until a skewer comes out clean when inserted into the centre of the cake. Leave in the tin for 30 minutes before turning out onto a wire rack to cool. If desired, combine a little extra cinnamon and sugar and sprinkle over the apple.

NUTRITION PER SERVE
Fat 17.5 g; Protein 5 g; Carbohydrate 47 g; Dietary Fibre 1.5 g; Cholesterol 96.5 mg; 1515 kJ (360 cal)

1

2

3

PINEAPPLE UPSIDE-DOWN CAKE

Preparation time: 15 minutes
Total cooking time: 40 minutes
Serves 6–8

20 g unsalted butter, melted
2 tablespoons firmly packed soft brown sugar
440 g can pineapple rings in natural juice
90 g unsalted butter, extra, softened
1/2 cup (125 g) caster sugar
2 eggs, lightly beaten
1 teaspoon vanilla essence
1 cup (125 g) self-raising flour

1 Preheat the oven to moderate 180°C (350°F/Gas 4). Grease a 20 cm ring tin. Pour the melted butter into the base of the tin and tip to evenly coat. Sprinkle with the brown sugar. Drain the pineapple and reserve 1/3 cup (80 ml) of the juice. Cut the pineapple slices in half and arrange on the base.

2 Beat the extra butter and the caster sugar with electric beaters until light and creamy. Gradually add the egg, beating well after each addition. Add the vanilla essence and beat until combined. Fold in the flour alternately with the reserved juice, using a metal spoon.

3 Spoon the mixture evenly over the pineapple and smooth the surface. Bake for 35–40 minutes, or until a skewer comes out clean when inserted into the centre of the cake. Leave in the tin for 10 minutes before turning out onto a wire rack to cool.

NUTRITION PER SERVE (8)
Fat 12.5 g; Protein 4 g; Carbohydrate 35.5 g; Dietary Fibre 1.5 g; Cholesterol 80 mg; 1120 kJ (270 cal)

1

2

3

CHESTNUT CAKE

Preparation time: 15 minutes
Total cooking time: 50 minutes
Serves 6–8

125 g unsalted butter, softened
1 cup (250 g) caster sugar
1 teaspoon vanilla essence
150 g unsweetened chestnut purée, crumbled
3 eggs, lightly beaten
1/3 cup (80 ml) milk
1 1/4 cups (155 g) self-raising flour
1 teaspoon baking powder

1 Preheat the oven to moderate 180°C (350°F/Gas 4). Grease a 20 cm ring tin and line the base with baking paper. Beat the butter, sugar and vanilla essence with electric beaters until light and creamy. Add the chestnut purée and beat for 1 minute, or until just combined.

2 Gradually add the egg, beating well after each addition. Fold in the milk, flour and baking powder all at once and stir with a wooden spoon until the ingredients are just combined—do not overbeat. Spoon the mixture into the prepared tin and smooth the surface. Bake for 45–50 minutes, or until a skewer comes out clean when inserted into the centre of the cake. Leave in the tin for 5 minutes before turning onto a wire rack to cool.

NUTRITION PER SERVE (8)
Fat 15.5 g; Protein 5 g; Carbohydrate 50.5 g; Dietary Fibre 1 g; Cholesterol 109 mg; 1495 kJ (355 cal)

COOK'S FILE
Note: Drizzle with Chocolate glaze (see page 12).

1

2

MELT AND MIX CAKES

SEMOLINA BERRY CAKE

Preparation time: 10 minutes
Total cooking time: 50 minutes
Serves 8

- 1 1/2 cups (185 g) fine semolina
- 3/4 cup (185 g) caster sugar
- 2 teaspoons baking powder
- 180 g unsalted butter, melted
- 1 teaspoon vanilla essence
- 1 cup (250 g) plain yoghurt
- 150 g fresh raspberries (or thawed frozen) (see Note)
- 1/2 cup (45 g) flaked almonds

1 Preheat the oven to moderate 180°C (350°F/Gas 4). Grease a deep 20 cm round cake tin and line the base with baking paper. Place the semolina, sugar and baking powder in a bowl. Combine the melted butter, vanilla and yoghurt and add to the dry ingredients, stirring until smooth and just combined.
2 Spoon half the mixture into the cake tin and smooth the surface. Scatter the raspberries evenly over the top, then spoon on the remaining mixture. Press the almonds into the top of the cake mixture to cover. Bake for 50 minutes, or until a skewer comes out clean when inserted into the centre of the cake. Leave in the tin for 10 minutes before carefully inverting onto a wire rack to cool.

NUTRITION PER SERVE
Fat 22.5 g; Protein 6 g; Carbohydrate 46.5 g; Dietary Fibre 2.5 g; Cholesterol 60.5 mg; 1710 kJ (410 cal)

COOK'S FILE
Note: If using frozen raspberries, pat dry well to remove any excess moisture.

1

2

PISTACHIO PLUM CAKE

Preparation time: 15 minutes
Total cooking time: 1 hour 10 minutes
Serves 8–10

- 1 1/2 cups (185 g) self-raising flour
- 1 1/2 teaspoons ground cinnamon
- 100 g unsalted butter, melted
- 1 cup (230 g) firmly packed soft brown sugar
- 3 eggs, lightly beaten
- 1/3 cup (50 g) pistachio kernels, finely chopped
- 825 g can seeded plums in syrup, drained (reserving the juice) and chopped
- 2 teaspoons cornflour

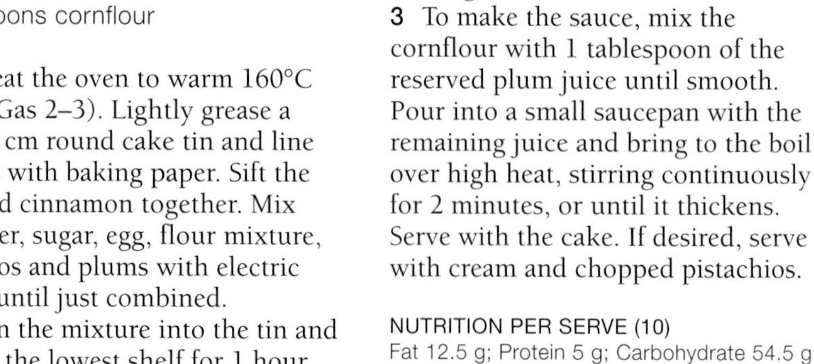

1 Preheat the oven to warm 160°C (315°F/Gas 2–3). Lightly grease a deep 20 cm round cake tin and line the base with baking paper. Sift the flour and cinnamon together. Mix the butter, sugar, egg, flour mixture, pistachios and plums with electric beaters until just combined.

2 Spoon the mixture into the tin and bake on the lowest shelf for 1 hour 10 minutes, or until a skewer comes out clean when inserted into the centre of the cake. Leave in the tin for 10 minutes before carefully turning onto a wire rack to cool.

3 To make the sauce, mix the cornflour with 1 tablespoon of the reserved plum juice until smooth. Pour into a small saucepan with the remaining juice and bring to the boil over high heat, stirring continuously for 2 minutes, or until it thickens. Serve with the cake. If desired, serve with cream and chopped pistachios.

NUTRITION PER SERVE (10)
Fat 12.5 g; Protein 5 g; Carbohydrate 54.5 g; Dietary Fibre 2 g; Cholesterol 79 mg; 1440 kJ (345 cal)

1

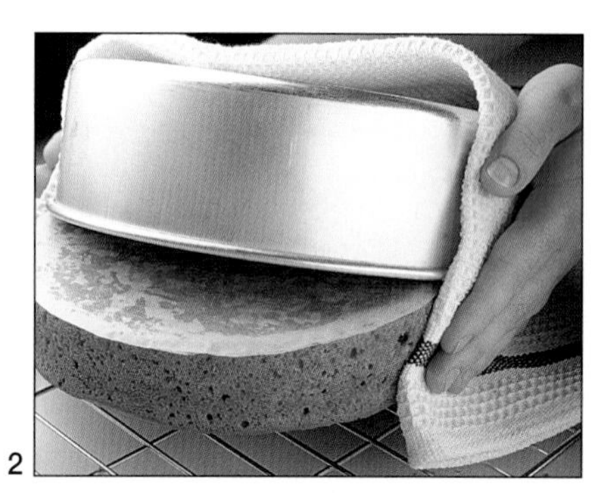

2

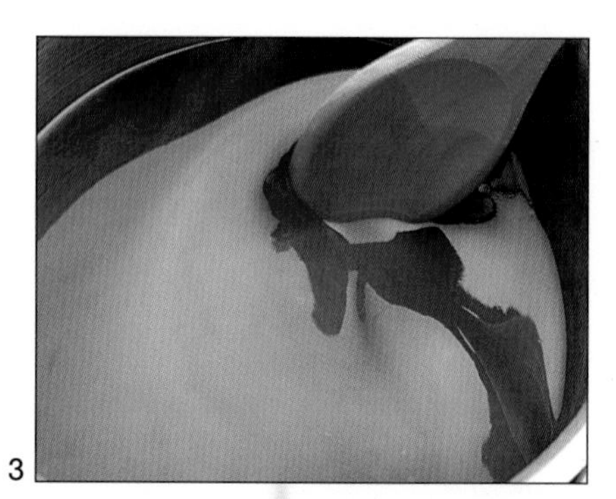

3

SAFFRON SPICE

Preparation time: 10 minutes
Total cooking time: 1 hour
Serves 8

- 1 cup (250 ml) freshly squeezed orange juice
- 1 tablespoon finely grated orange rind
- 1/4 teaspoon saffron threads
- 3 eggs
- 1 1/4 cups (155 g) icing sugar
- 2 cups (250 g) self-raising flour
- 2 cups (370 g) ground almonds
- 125 g unsalted butter, melted

1 Preheat the oven to moderate 180°C (350°F/Gas 4). Lightly grease a 22 cm round cake tin and line the base with baking paper. Combine the orange juice, rind and saffron in a small saucepan and bring to the boil. Lower the heat and simmer for 1 minute. Leave to cool.

2 Beat the eggs and icing sugar with electric beaters until light and creamy. Fold in the sifted flour, almonds, orange juice mixture and butter with a metal spoon until just combined and the mixture is just smooth. Spoon the mixture into the prepared tin.

3 Bake for 1 hour, or until a skewer comes out clean when inserted into the centre of the cake. Leave in the tin for 15 minutes before turning onto a wire rack to cool. If desired, dust with a little extra icing sugar and serve with thick cream.

NUTRITION PER SERVE
Fat 31 g; Protein 10.5 g; Carbohydrate 40 g; Dietary Fibre 3.5 g; Cholesterol 107 mg; 1970 kJ (470 cal)

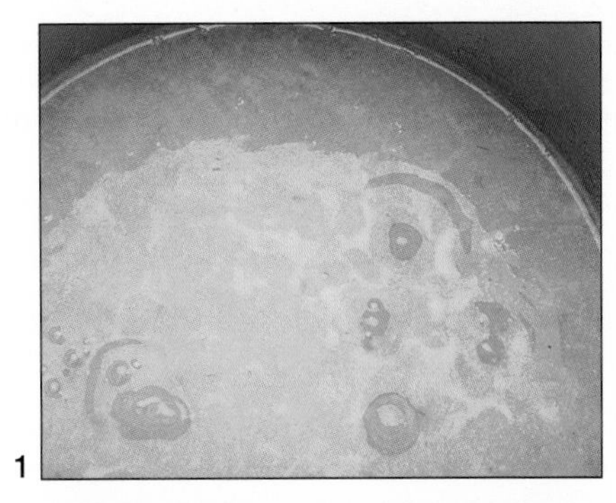
1

2

3

GOLDEN GINGER PEAR CAKE

Preparation time: 10 minutes
Total cooking time: 1 hour 35 minutes
Serves 8

- 1/2 cup (175 g) golden syrup
- 2 cups (250 g) self-raising flour
- 2 1/2 teaspoons ground ginger
- 3/4 cup (165 g) firmly packed soft brown sugar
- 2 pears (about 200 g), peeled, halved and thinly sliced
- 3 eggs, lightly beaten
- 1/2 cup (125 ml) buttermilk
- 150 g unsalted butter, chopped

1 Preheat the oven to moderate 180°C (350°F/Gas 4). Grease a deep 18 cm round cake tin and line the base with baking paper. Pour half of the golden syrup over the base of the tin, spreading evenly with a metal spoon which has been run under hot water.

2 Sift the flour and ground ginger into a bowl. Add the sugar and pear, then the egg, buttermilk and 125 g of the butter, melted, and stir until just combined and smooth. Spoon the mixture into the prepared tin and bake for 1 hour 30 minutes, or until a skewer comes out clean when inserted into the centre of the cake. Leave in the tin for 10 minutes, then carefully invert onto a serving plate.

3 Heat the remaining golden syrup and the remaining butter in a small saucepan over low heat until the butter has melted. Spoon the sauce evenly over the cake and serve warm. If desired, serve with ice cream or cream.

NUTRITION PER SERVE
Fat 18 g; Protein 6.5 g; Carbohydrate 65.5 g; Dietary Fibre 2 g; Cholesterol 117 mg; 1840 kJ (440 cal)

1

2

3

HONEY, BANANA AND MACADAMIA CAKE

Preparation time: 10 minutes
Total cooking time: 1 hour 15 minutes
Serves 8–10

125 g unsalted butter, chopped
1 1/4 cups (440 g) honey
2 1/2 cups (310 g) self-raising flour
1 1/2 teaspoons mixed spice
3 or 4 large carrots (220 g), coarsely grated
1 large ripe banana, mashed
3/4 cup (120 g) macadamia nuts, chopped
3 eggs, lightly beaten

1 Preheat the oven to moderate 180°C (350°F/Gas 4). Grease a 26 cm round cake tin and line the base with baking paper. Melt the butter and honey in a small saucepan, stirring until combined. Cool.

2 Sift the flour and mixed spice into a large bowl. Add the carrot, banana, macadamias, egg and honey mixture, stirring until the mixture is just combined and smooth. Spoon the mixture into the prepared tin and bake for 1 hour 10 minutes, or until a skewer comes out clean when inserted into the centre of the cake. Leave in the tin for 15 minutes before carefully turning out onto a wire rack to cool.

NUTRITION PER SERVE (10)
Fat 20 g; Protein 6.5 g; Carbohydrate 61.5 g; Dietary Fibre 3 g; Cholesterol 85.5 mg; 1855 kJ (445 cal)

COOK'S FILE
Note: Cover with Ricotta honey icing (see page 8).

1

2

INDIVIDUAL STICKY DATE CAKES

Preparation time: 10 minutes
Total cooking time: 25 minutes
Makes 6

- 1 1/2 cups (270 g) pitted dates, chopped
- 1 teaspoon bicarbonate of soda
- 150 g unsalted butter, chopped
- 1 1/2 cups (185 g) self-raising flour
- 265 g firmly packed soft brown sugar
- 2 eggs, lightly beaten
- 2 tablespoons golden syrup
- 3/4 cup (185 ml) cream

1 Preheat the oven to moderate 180°C (350°F/Gas 4). Grease six 1 cup (250 ml) muffin holes. Place the dates and 1 cup (250 ml) water in a saucepan, bring to the boil, then remove from the heat and stir in the bicarbonate of soda. Add 60 g of the butter and stir until dissolved. Sift the flour into a large bowl, add 2/3 cup (125 g) of the sugar and stir. Make a well in the centre, add the date mixture and egg and stir until just combined. Spoon the mixture evenly into the prepared holes and bake for 20 minutes, or until a skewer comes out clean when inserted into the centre.

2 To make the sauce, place the golden syrup, cream, the remaining butter and the remaining sugar in a small saucepan and stir over low heat for 3–4 minutes, or until the sugar has dissolved. Bring to the boil, then reduce the heat and simmer, stirring occasionally, for 2 minutes. To serve, turn the cakes onto serving plates, pierce the cakes a few times with a skewer and drizzle with the sauce. Serve with ice cream, if desired.

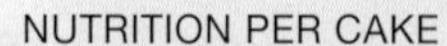

NUTRITION PER CAKE
Fat 36 g; Protein 7 g; Carbohydrate 103 g; Dietary Fibre 5.5 g; Cholesterol 166 mg; 3115 kJ (745 cal)

1

2

RHUBARB YOGHURT CAKE

Preparation time: 10 minutes
Total cooking time: 1 hour
Serves 8

- 1 1/2 cups (150 g) finely sliced fresh rhubarb
- 2 1/2 cups (310 g) self-raising flour, sifted
- 1 cup (250 g) caster sugar
- 1 teaspoon vanilla essence
- 2 eggs, lightly beaten
- 1/2 cup (125 g) plain yoghurt
- 1 tablespoon rosewater
- 125 g unsalted butter, melted

1 Preheat the oven to moderate 180°C (350°F/Gas 4). Lightly grease a 23 cm round cake tin and line the base with baking paper. Combine the rhubarb, flour and sugar in a bowl.

2 Add the vanilla, egg, yoghurt, rosewater and melted butter, stirring until the mixture is just combined. Spoon the mixture into the cake tin and bake for 1 hour, or until a skewer comes out clean when inserted into the centre of the cake. Leave in the tin for 15 minutes before turning out onto a wire rack. Serve with yoghurt or cream, if desired.

NUTRITION PER SERVE
Fat 15 g; Protein 8 g; Carbohydrate 71 g; Dietary Fibre 2.5 g; Cholesterol 87 mg; 1880 kJ (450 cal)

1

2

APPLE AND PECAN CAKE

Preparation time: 15 minutes
Total cooking time: 1 hour 10 minutes
Serves 8

2 1/2 cups (310 g) self-raising flour
1 1/2 teaspoons ground cinnamon
3/4 cup (185 g) sugar
2 Granny Smith apples (about 340 g), peeled and diced
1/2 cup (50 g) pecans, chopped
2 eggs, lightly beaten
1/2 cup (125 ml) milk
15 g unsalted butter, melted

1 Preheat the oven to moderate 180°C (350°F/Gas 4). Lightly grease a 23 cm round cake tin and line the base with baking paper. Combine the flour, cinnamon, sugar, apple and pecans in a bowl.
2 Add the egg, milk and melted butter, stirring until the mixture is just combined and smooth.
3 Spoon into the prepared tin and bake for 1 hour 10 minutes, or until a skewer comes out clean when inserted into the centre of the cake. Leave in the tin for 15 minutes before carefully turning out onto a wire rack to cool. If desired, dust with icing sugar and serve with thick cream or yoghurt.

NUTRITION PER SERVE
Fat 8.5 g; Protein 8 g; Carbohydrate 63.5 g; Dietary Fibre 3.5 g; Cholesterol 52 mg; 1490 kJ (355 cal)

COOK'S FILE
Note: The surface of this cake is quite rough and textured.

1

2

3

INDIVIDUAL MILK CHOCOLATE CAKES

Preparation time: 15 minutes
Total cooking time: 25 minutes
Makes 12

75 g unsalted butter
75 g milk chocolate, chopped
1/3 cup (80 g) firmly packed brown sugar
2 eggs, lightly beaten
1/2 cup (60 g) self-raising flour, sifted

Ganache
80 g milk chocolate, chopped
2 tablespoons thick cream

1 Preheat the oven to warm 160°C (315°F/Gas 2–3). Line a flat-bottomed 12-hole cupcake tray with paper patty cases. Place the butter and chocolate in a heatproof bowl and place over a saucepan of simmering water—ensure the base of the bowl doesn't touch the water. Stir until melted and combined. Remove the bowl from the heat, add the sugar and egg and mix. Stir in the flour.

2 Transfer the mixture to a measuring jug and pour into the patty cases. Bake for 20–25 minutes, or until cooked. Leave in the tin for 10 minutes before transferring to a wire rack to cool completely.

3 To make the ganache, place the chocolate and cream in a heatproof bowl. Place over a saucepan of simmering water—ensure the base of the bowl doesn't touch the water. Once the chocolate has almost melted remove the bowl from the heat and stir until the remaining chocolate has melted and the mixture is smooth. Allow to cool for about 8 minutes, or until thickened slightly. Return the cakes to the cold patty tin, to keep them stable while you spread one heaped teaspoon of ganache over the top. If desired, decorate with gold cachous.

NUTRITION PER CAKE
Fat 11 g; Protein 2.5 g; Carbohydrate 18 g; Dietary Fibre 0.5 g; Cholesterol 52 mg; 740 kJ (175 cal)

COOK'S FILE
Note: If desired, you can use decorative foil patty cases—this will give you a larger cupcake.

1

2

3

BUTTER ALMOND TORTE

Preparation time: 15 minutes
Total cooking time: 1 hour 10 minutes
Serves 8–10

120 g unsalted butter, chopped
90 ml milk
2 eggs
1 teaspoon vanilla essence
2 cups (250 g) caster sugar
135 g plain flour
2 teaspoons baking powder
100 g slivered almonds

1 Preheat the oven to moderate 180°C (350°F/Gas 4). Line the base of a 22 cm springform tin with foil and lightly grease the base and side. Heat 60 g of the butter and 1/3 cup (80 ml) milk in a small saucepan until the butter has melted.

2 Beat the eggs, vanilla and 3/4 cup (185 g) of the sugar with electric beaters until thick and creamy. Stir in the butter and milk mixture. Sift in 1 cup (125 g) of the flour and the baking powder and stir to combine—the mixture will be thin. Pour into the tin and bake for 50 minutes.

3 Melt the remaining butter in a small saucepan. Stir in the almonds with the remaining sugar, flour and milk and stir until combined. Quickly spoon the topping onto the cake—the centre will still be uncooked—starting from the outside edges and avoid piling the topping in the centre. Return to the oven for a further 10–15 minutes, or until golden and cooked through. Cool in the tin before inverting onto a wire rack.

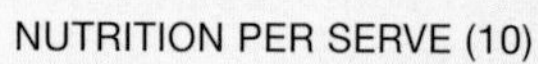

NUTRITION PER SERVE (10)
Fat 17 g; Protein 5 g; Carbohydrate 36 g; Dietary Fibre 1.5 g; Cholesterol 68 mg; 1305 kJ (310 cal)

COOK'S FILE
Note: This torte is great served as a dessert with whipped cream. Store in an airtight container for 4 days.

1

2

3

GINGERBREAD APRICOT UPSIDE-DOWN CAKE

Preparation time: 15 minutes
Total cooking time: 45 minutes
Serves 6

200 g glacé apricots
175 g unsalted butter
30 g pecans, finely chopped
3/4 cup (165 g) firmly packed soft brown sugar
1/4 cup (90 g) golden syrup
1 1/2 cups (185 g) self-raising flour
3 teaspoons ground ginger
1/2 teaspoon ground nutmeg

1 Preheat the oven to moderate 180°C (350°F/Gas 4). Grease and flour the base of a deep 20 cm round cake tin, shaking out the excess flour. Arrange the apricots around the base of the tin, cut-side up. Melt the butter in a small saucepan over low heat. Transfer 1 tablespoon of the melted butter to a small bowl. Add the pecans and 1/4 cup (55 g) of the sugar and mix well. Sprinkle the mixture over the apricots.

2 Add the golden syrup and 1/2 cup (125 ml) water to the saucepan of melted butter and stir over medium heat until well combined. Sift the flour and spices in a bowl, then stir in the remaining sugar. Pour in the golden syrup mixture and mix well. Spoon the mixture over the apricots and smooth the surface. Bake for 35–40 minutes, or until a skewer comes out clean when inserted into the centre of the cake. Leave in the tin for 15 minutes before turning out onto a wire rack to cool.

NUTRITION PER SERVE
Fat 28 g; Protein 4 g; Carbohydrate 82.5 g; Dietary Fibre 2 g; Cholesterol 74.5 mg; 2445 kJ (585 cal)

COOK'S FILE
Note: Keeps for 4 days in an airtight cake tin.

1

2

RICH DARK CHOCOLATE CAKE

Preparation time: 15 minutes
Total cooking time: 1 hour 40 minutes
Serves 10–12

185 g unsalted butter, chopped
250 g dark chocolate bits
1 3/4 cups (215 g) self-raising flour
1/3 cup (40 g) cocoa powder
1 1/2 cups (375 g) caster sugar
3 eggs, lightly beaten

Chocolate topping
20 g unsalted butter, chopped
125 g dark chocolate, chopped

1 Preheat the oven to warm 160°C (315°F/Gas 2–3). Grease a 22 cm springform tin and line the base with baking paper. Place the butter and chocolate bits in a small heatproof bowl and melt, stirring frequently, over a saucepan of simmering water—ensure the base of the bowl doesn't touch the water.
2 Sift the flour and cocoa into a large bowl. Combine the melted butter and chocolate mixture, sugar and egg, then add 1 cup (250 ml) of water and mix well. Add to the flour and cocoa and stir until well combined. Pour the mixture into the prepared tin and bake for 1 hour 30 minutes, or until a skewer comes out clean when inserted into the centre of the cake. Leave in the tin for 15 minutes before turning out onto a wire rack to cool.
3 To make the chocolate topping, place the butter and chocolate pieces in a small heatproof bowl and melt, stirring frequently, over a saucepan of simmering water—ensure the base of the bowl doesn't touch the water. Spread over the cooled cake in a swirl pattern.

NUTRITION PER SERVE (12)
Fat 25 g; Protein 5.5 g; Carbohydrate 64.5 g; Dietary Fibre 1 g; Cholesterol 88.5 mg; 2060 kJ (490 cal)

1

2

3

RUM AND RAISIN CAKE

Preparation time: 15 minutes + 10 minutes soaking
Total cooking time: 45 minutes
Serves 8

1 cup (160 g) raisins
1/4 cup (60 ml) dark rum
1 1/2 cups (185 g) self-raising flour
150 g unsalted butter, chopped
3/4 cup (140 g) lightly packed soft brown sugar
3 eggs, lightly beaten

1 Preheat the oven to moderate 180°C (350°F/Gas 4). Grease a deep 20 cm round cake tin and line the base with baking paper. Soak the raisins and rum in a small bowl for 10 minutes. Sift the flour into a large bowl and make a well in the centre.

2 Melt the butter and sugar in a small saucepan over low heat, stirring until the sugar has dissolved. Remove from the heat. Combine with the rum and raisin mixture and add to the flour with the egg. Stir with a wooden spoon until combined—do not overbeat.

3 Spoon the mixture into the prepared tin and smooth the surface. Bake for 40 minutes, or until a skewer comes out clean when inserted into the centre of the cake. Delicious served with ice cream.

NUTRITION PER SERVE
Fat 18 g; Protein 5 g; Carbohydrate 44.5 g; Dietary Fibre 1.5 g; Cholesterol 114.5 mg; 1540 kJ (370 cal)

1

2

3

ORANGE AND LEMON SYRUP CAKE

Preparation time: 15 minutes
Total cooking time: 1 hour 30 minutes
Serves 10–12

3 lemons
3 oranges
250 g unsalted butter, chilled and chopped
$2^3/4$ cups (685 g) caster sugar
6 eggs, lightly beaten
$1^1/2$ cups (375 ml) milk
3 cups (375 g) self-raising flour, sifted

1 Preheat the oven to warm 160°C (315°F/Gas 2–3). Grease a 24 cm springform tin and line the base and side with baking paper. Finely grate the rind from the lemons and oranges to give 3 tablespoons of each. Squeeze the lemons and oranges to give 3/4 cup (185 ml) juice from each. Heat the butter, 2 cups (500 g) of the sugar, 1 tablespoon of the lemon rind and 1 tablespoon of the orange rind in a saucepan over low heat, stirring until melted and combined. Transfer to a bowl.

2 Add half the egg, 3/4 cup (185 ml) of the milk and $1^1/2$ cups (185 g) of the flour to the bowl, beating with electric beaters until just combined. Add the remaining egg, milk and flour and beat until smooth—do not overmix. Pour into the tin and bake for 1 hour 15 minutes, or until a skewer comes out clean when inserted into the centre of the cake—cover with foil if it browns too much. Cool in the tin.

3 To make the syrup, combine the lemon and orange juices, remaining lemon and orange rinds, remaining sugar and 1/2 cup (125 ml) water in a saucepan and stir over low heat until the sugar has dissolved. Increase the heat and bring to the boil for 10 minutes, or until it thickens and reduces slightly. Pour the hot syrup over the cool cake. Cool in the tin for 10 minutes then remove.

NUTRITION PER SERVE (12)
Fat 21 g; Protein 7.5 g; Carbohydrate 82.5 g; Dietary Fibre 1.5 g; Cholesterol 147.5 mg; 2265 kJ (540 cal)

COOK'S FILE
Note: Add some orange zest to the syrup in the last 10 minutes, for garnish.

1

2

3

CUSTARD BUTTER CAKE

Preparation time: 15 minutes
Total cooking time: 40 minutes
Serves 8–10

1 cup (125 g) self-raising flour
2/3 cup (85 g) custard powder
1/2 teaspoon bicarbonate of soda
125 g unsalted butter, chopped
3/4 cup (185 g) caster sugar
3 eggs, lightly beaten
1/4 cup (60 ml) buttermilk

1 Preheat the oven to moderate 180°C (350°F/Gas 4). Grease a deep 20 cm square cake tin and line the base with baking paper. Sift the flour, custard powder and bicarbonate of soda into a large bowl and make a well in the centre.

2 Melt the butter and sugar in a small saucepan over low heat, stirring until the sugar has dissolved. Remove from the heat. Add the butter mixture and combined egg and buttermilk to the dry ingredients and stir with a wooden spoon until combined—do not overbeat. Spoon the mixture into the prepared tin and smooth the surface. Bake for 35 minutes, or until a skewer comes out clean when inserted into the centre of the cake. Leave in the tin to cool.

NUTRITION PER SERVE (10)
Fat 12 g; Protein 3.5 g; Carbohydrate 35 g; Dietary Fibre 0.5 g; Cholesterol 86 mg; 1085 kJ (260 cal)

COOK'S FILE
Note: To dress up this cake, ice with White chocolate cream cheese icing (see page 6), then decorate with crystalised violets and silver cachous.
Storage: Un-iced, this cake will keep for up to 4 days in an airtight container.

1

2

JAFFA CAKE

Preparation time: 10 minutes
Total cooking time: 50 minutes
Serves 8–10

1 1/3 cups (165 g) self-raising flour
1/4 cup (30 g) cocoa powder
1 cup (250 g) sugar
2 eggs, lightly beaten
2/3 cup (170 ml) milk
125 g unsalted butter, melted
1 tablespoon finely grated orange rind

1 Preheat the oven to moderate 180°C (350°F/Gas 4). Lightly grease a deep 20 cm round cake tin and line the base with baking paper. Sift the flour and cocoa into a large bowl, then stir in the sugar.

2 Add the egg, milk, melted butter and orange rind and beat with electric beaters for 2 minutes, or until well combined and smooth.

3 Pour into the prepared tin and bake for 45–50 minutes, or until a skewer comes out clean when inserted into the centre of the cake. Turn out onto a wire rack. If desired, cover with chocolate or orange icing.

NUTRITION PER SERVE (10)
Fat 12.5 g; Protein 4 g; Carbohydrate 39 g; Dietary Fibre 1 g; Cholesterol 70.5 mg; 1170 kJ (280 cal)

1

2

3

ESPRESSO COFFEE BARS

Preparation time: 15 minutes + 15 minutes soaking
Total cooking time: 40 minutes
Serves 6–8

- 1/4 cup (20 g) finely ground espresso coffee beans (see Notes)
- 2 cups (250 g) self-raising flour, sifted
- 1/3 cup (40 g) finely chopped pecan nuts
- 150 g unsalted butter, chopped
- 3/4 cup (140 g) lightly packed soft brown sugar
- 2 eggs, lightly beaten

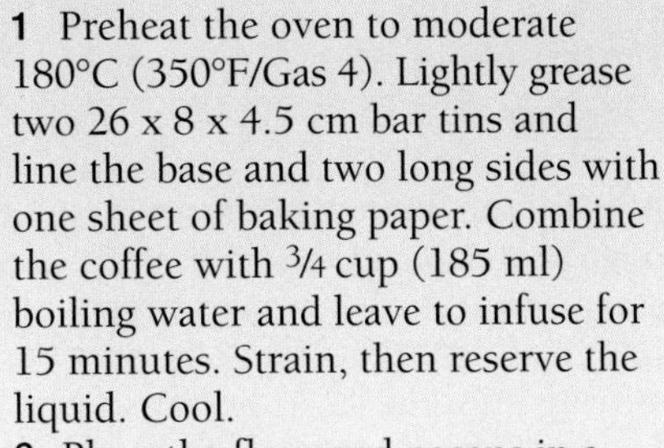

1 Preheat the oven to moderate 180°C (350°F/Gas 4). Lightly grease two 26 x 8 x 4.5 cm bar tins and line the base and two long sides with one sheet of baking paper. Combine the coffee with 3/4 cup (185 ml) boiling water and leave to infuse for 15 minutes. Strain, then reserve the liquid. Cool.

2 Place the flour and pecans in a large bowl and make a well in the centre. Melt the butter and sugar in a small saucepan over low heat, stirring until the sugar has dissolved. Combine the egg and reserved coffee liquid. Add both the butter and the egg mixtures to the dry ingredients and stir with a wooden spoon until combined—do not overbeat.

3 Divide the mixture evenly between the tins and smooth the surface. Bake for 35 minutes, or until a skewer comes out clean when inserted into the centre of the cake. Turn onto a wire rack to cool.

NUTRITION PER SERVE (8)
Fat 21 g; Protein 5.5 g; Carbohydrate 39.5 g; Dietary Fibre 2 g; Cholesterol 92 mg; 1520 kJ (365 cal)

COOK'S FILE
Notes: You can dissolve 1 tablespoon instant coffee powder in the boiling water instead of infusing ground beans. Decorate with Coffee glacé icing (see page 8) and pecan nuts, if desired.

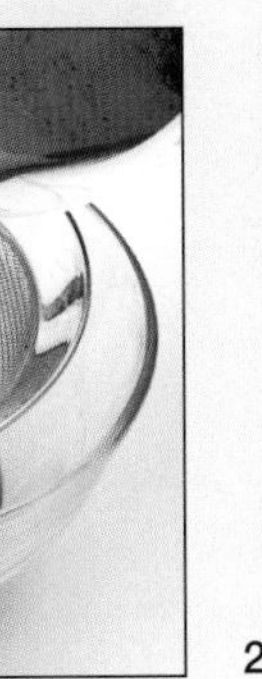
1

2

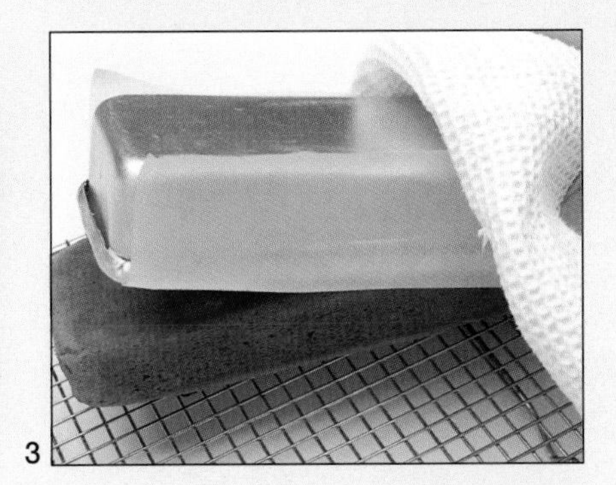
3

APRICOT, SOUR CREAM AND COCONUT CAKE

Preparation time: 15 minutes
Total cooking time: 45 minutes
Serves 6–8

1 1/2 cups (185 g) self-raising flour, sifted
1/2 cup (45 g) desiccated coconut
125 g unsalted butter
1 cup (250 g) caster sugar
2 eggs, lightly beaten
1 cup (250 ml) apricot nectar
1/2 cup (125 g) sour cream

1 Preheat the oven to moderate 180°C (350°F/Gas 4). Lightly grease and flour a 23 cm fluted baba tin and shake off the excess flour.
2 Place the flour and coconut in a large bowl and make a well in the centre. Melt the butter and sugar in a small saucepan over low heat, stirring until the sugar has dissolved. Remove from the heat. Whisk the combined egg and apricot nectar into the sour cream. Add both the butter and the egg mixtures to the dry ingredients and stir with a wooden spoon until combined—do not overbeat.
3 Pour the mixture into the tin. Bake for 40 minutes, or until a skewer comes out clean when inserted into the centre of the cake. Turn out onto a wire rack to cool.

NUTRITION PER SERVE (8)
Fat 24.5 g; Protein 5 g; Carbohydrate 53 g; Dietary Fibre 1.5 g; Cholesterol 106.5 mg; 1845 kJ (440 cal)

COOK'S FILE
Note: Decorate with Orange glacé icing (see page 9) and glacé orange rind, if desired. Store for up to 3 days in an airtight container in a cool, dry place.

1

2

3

PEAR UPSIDE-DOWN CAKE

Preparation time: 15 minutes
Total cooking time: 55 minutes
Serves 6–8

2 tablespoons firmly packed soft brown sugar
425 g can pear halves in syrup
2 cups (250 g) self-raising flour
125 g unsalted butter
3/4 cup (185 g) caster sugar
2 eggs, lightly beaten

1 Preheat the oven to moderate 180°C (350°F/Gas 4). Grease a 21 x 14 x 7 cm loaf tin and line the base with baking paper. Sprinkle the brown sugar evenly over the base of the tin. Drain the pears and reserve the syrup. Cut the pears in half and arrange, cut-side down, over the base of the tin.
2 Sift the flour into a large bowl and make a well in the centre. Melt the butter and caster sugar in a small saucepan over low heat, stirring until the sugar has dissolved. Remove from the heat. Combine the egg with the reserved syrup. Add both the butter and the egg mixtures to the flour and stir with a wooden spoon until combined—do not overbeat. Spoon the mixture over the pears and smooth the surface. Bake for 50 minutes, or until a skewer comes out clean when inserted into the centre of the cake. Leave in the tin for 15 minutes before turning onto a wire rack to cool.

NUTRITION PER SERVE (8)
Fat 14.5 g; Protein 5 g; Carbohydrate 56.5 g; Dietary Fibre 2 g; Cholesterol 84.5 mg; 1550 kJ (370 cal)

COOK'S FILE
Note: If the pears are too large, cut them in half lengthwise.
Hint: Be sure to allow the full standing time before turning out, or the pears may not adhere to the cake.

1

2

FOOD PROCESSOR CAKES

FLOURLESS ORANGE AND ALMOND CAKE

Preparation time: 15 minutes
Total cooking time: 1 hour 30 minutes
Serves 8

2 oranges
1 1/2 cups (280 g) ground almonds
1 cup (250 g) caster sugar
1 teaspoon baking powder
1 teaspoon vanilla essence
1 teaspoon Cointreau
6 eggs, lightly beaten
icing sugar, to dust

1 Place the whole oranges in a saucepan, cover with water and place a small plate on top to keep the oranges submerged. Gradually bring to the boil, then reduce the heat and simmer for 40 minutes, or until very soft. Preheat the oven to moderate 180°C (350°F/Gas 4). Grease a 23 cm springform tin and line the base with baking paper.

2 Cut the oranges into quarters and leave to cool. Remove any pips, then blend in a food processor until very smooth. Add the ground almonds, sugar, baking powder, vanilla essence and Cointreau and, using the pulse button, process until just combined. Add the egg and process again until just combined—do not overprocess. Pour into the prepared tin and bake for 50 minutes, or until firm and the cake leaves the side of the tin. Leave to cool in the tin. Dust with icing sugar to serve.

NUTRITION PER SERVE
Fat 14 g; Protein 9 g; Carbohydrate 35 g; Dietary Fibre 2.5 g; Cholesterol 135 mg; 1240 kJ (295 cal)

COOK'S FILE
Note: This makes a great dessert cake served with fruit and cream.

1

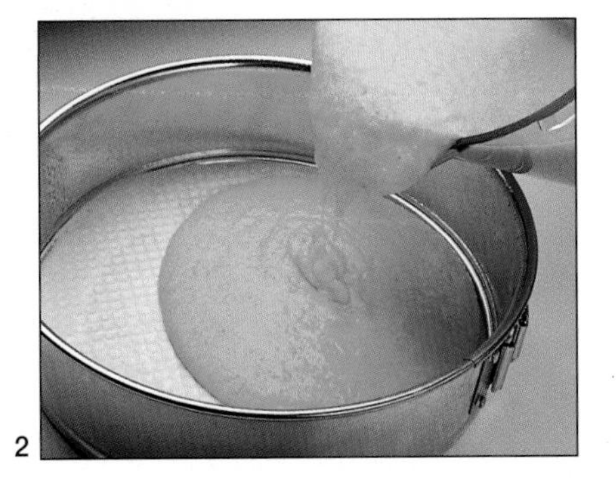
2

PLUM CRUMBLE CAKE

Preparation time: 15 minutes
Total cooking time: 50 minutes
Serves 8

3/4 cup (165 g) demerara sugar
2 cups (250 g) self-raising flour
150 g unsalted butter
1 egg
825 g can plums in syrup, drained and thinly sliced
1 1/2 teaspoons ground cinnamon
2/3 cup (100 g) blanched almonds, chopped

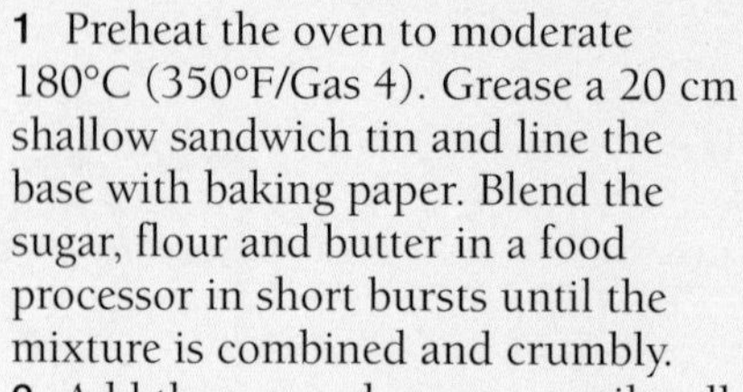

1 Preheat the oven to moderate 180°C (350°F/Gas 4). Grease a 20 cm shallow sandwich tin and line the base with baking paper. Blend the sugar, flour and butter in a food processor in short bursts until the mixture is combined and crumbly.
2 Add the egg and process until well combined. Press half the mixture onto the base of the prepared tin. Arrange the plum slices evenly over the dough, then sprinkle with the cinnamon.
3 Knead the almonds lightly into the remaining dough, then press onto the plum layer. Bake for 50 minutes, or until a skewer comes out clean when inserted into the centre of the cake. Leave in the tin for 15 minutes before carefully turning out onto a wire rack to cool slightly. Delicious served warm with thick cream.

NUTRITION PER SERVE
Fat 23.5 g; Protein 7 g; Carbohydrate 57 g; Dietary Fibre 4 g; Cholesterol 69.5 mg; 1935 kJ (460 cal)

1

2

3

BLUEBERRY SHORTCAKE

Preparation time: 15 minutes
Total cooking time: 1 hour
Serves 8–10

3/4 cup (100 g) whole hazelnuts
2 1/4 cups (280 g) self-raising flour
1 1/2 teaspoons ground cinnamon
3/4 cup (165 g) demerara sugar
150 g unsalted butter, chopped
2 eggs
1/2 cup (160 g) blueberry jam
1 tablespoon demarara sugar, extra

1 Preheat the oven to moderate 180°C (350°F/Gas 4). Grease a deep 20 cm round cake tin and line the base with baking paper. Spread the hazelnuts on a baking tray and bake for 5–10 minutes, or until lightly golden. Place in a clean tea towel and rub together to remove the skins, then roughly chop.

2 Mix the flour, cinnamon, sugar, butter and half the hazelnuts in a food processor in short bursts until finely chopped. Add the eggs and process until well combined. Press half the mixture onto the base of the tin, then spread the jam evenly over the mixture.

3 Lightly knead the remaining hazelnuts into the remaining dough, then press evenly over the jam layer. Sprinkle the extra sugar over the top and bake for 50 minutes, or until a skewer comes out clean when inserted into the centre of the cake. Leave in the tin for 15 minutes before carefully turning out onto a wire rack to cool. If desired, garnish with fresh blueberries and serve with thick cream.

NUTRITION PER SERVE (10)
Fat 20 g; Protein 5.5 g; Carbohydrate 49.5 g; Dietary Fibre 2.5 g; Cholesterol 74.5 mg; 1640 kJ (390 cal)

1

2

3

CHOCOLATE CHERRY CAKE

Preparation time: 15 minutes
Total cooking time: 1 hour 10 minutes
Serves 8

- 200 g dark chocolate, chopped
- 250 g unsalted butter, chopped
- 1 cup (230 g) firmly packed soft brown sugar
- 1 teaspoon vanilla essence
- 1 1/4 cups (155 g) self-raising flour
- 1/2 cup (45 g) desiccated coconut
- 2 eggs
- 1 cup (180 g) pitted sour cherries, drained

1 Preheat the oven to warm 160°C (315°F/Gas 2–3). Grease a 23 cm round cake tin and line the base with baking paper. Place the chocolate, butter, sugar and vanilla in a heatproof bowl and melt, stirring occasionally, over a saucepan of simmering water until the chocolate has melted—ensure the base of the bowl doesn't touch the water. Sit the bowl in a sink of cold water to cool.

2 Combine the flour and coconut in a food processor. Add the chocolate mixture and eggs and process in short bursts until just combined. Add the cherries and process in one longish burst to just chop.

3 Pour the mixture into the tin and bake for 1 hour 10 minutes, or until a skewer comes out clean when inserted into the centre of the cake. Leave in the tin for 15 minutes before carefully turning out onto a wire rack to cool. If desired, dust with icing sugar and decorate with fresh cherries.

NUTRITION PER SERVE
Fat 38.5 g; Protein 5.5 g; Carbohydrate 60 g; Dietary Fibre 2 g; Cholesterol 123.5 mg; 2485 kJ (595 cal)

1

2

3

BANANA AND HONEY LOAF

Preparation time: 10 minutes
Total cooking time: 40 minutes
Serves 8

125 g unsalted butter, softened
3/4 cup (140 g) lightly packed soft brown sugar
2 eggs, lightly beaten
2 tablespoons honey
1 large (175 g) ripe banana, cut into chunks
1 1/2 cups (225 g) wholemeal self-raising flour
2 teaspoons ground cinnamon

1 Preheat the oven to moderate 180°C (350°F/Gas 4). Grease a 22 x 12 cm loaf tin. Combine the butter and sugar in a food processor for 1 minute, or until lighter in colour. Add the egg and process until combined. Place 1 tablespoon of the honey in a saucepan over low heat and warm for 1 minute, or until runny. Add to the food processor with the banana and blend until smooth. Add the flour and cinnamon and process until well combined.

2 Spoon evenly into the loaf tin and bake for 35–40 minutes, or until a skewer comes out clean when inserted into the centre of the cake. Leave in the tin for 5 minutes before turning out onto a wire rack to cool. Warm the remaining honey in a small saucepan over low heat for 1 minute, or until runny. Brush the warm cake with the warm honey. Serve warm or cool.

NUTRITION PER SERVE
Fat 14.5 g; Protein 5 g; Carbohydrate 40.5 g; Dietary Fibre 3 g; Cholesterol 85 mg; 1275 kJ (305 cal)

COOK'S FILE
Note: Alternatively, warm the honey in the microwave on Medium High (70%) for 30 seconds.
Variation: Fold 1/2 cup (60 g) chopped walnuts or pecans through the mixture before spooning into the loaf tin.

1

2

BABY COFFEE AND WALNUT SOUR CREAM CAKES

Preparation time: 15 minutes
Total cooking time: 20 minutes
Makes 24

- 3/4 cup (75 g) walnuts
- 2/3 cup (155 g) firmly packed soft brown sugar
- 125 g unsalted butter, softened
- 2 eggs, lightly beaten
- 1 cup (125 g) self-raising flour
- 1/3 cup (80 g) sour cream
- 1 tablespoon coffee and chicory essence

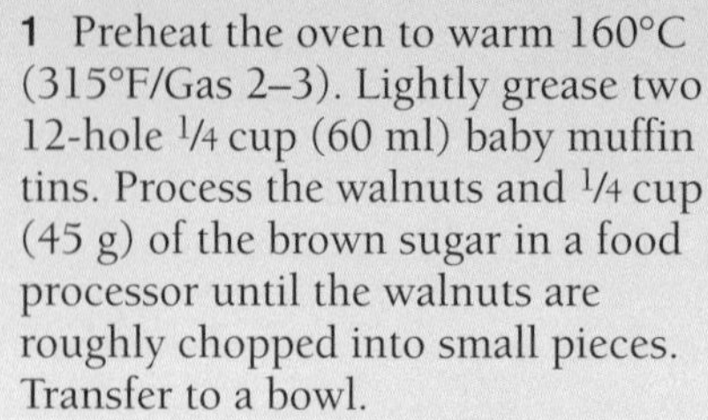

1 Preheat the oven to warm 160°C (315°F/Gas 2–3). Lightly grease two 12-hole 1/4 cup (60 ml) baby muffin tins. Process the walnuts and 1/4 cup (45 g) of the brown sugar in a food processor until the walnuts are roughly chopped into small pieces. Transfer to a bowl.

2 Cream the butter and remaining sugar together in the food processor until pale and creamy. With the motor running, gradually add the egg and process until smooth. Add the flour and blend until well mixed. Add the sour cream and essence and process until thoroughly mixed.

3 Spoon half a teaspoon of the walnut and sugar mixture into the base of each muffin hole, followed by a teaspoon of the cake mixture. Sprinkle a little more walnut mixture over the top, a little more cake mixture and top with the remaining walnut mixture. Bake for 20 minutes, or until risen and springy to the touch. Leave in the tins for 5 minutes. Remove the cakes using the handle of a teaspoon to loosen the side and base, then transfer to a wire rack to cool completely.

NUTRITION PER CAKE
Fat 8.5 g; Protein 1.5 g; Carbohydrate 11 g; Dietary Fibre 0.5 g; Cholesterol 32.5 mg; 510 kJ (120 cal)

1

2

3

PISTACHIO, YOGHURT AND CARDAMOM CAKE

Preparation time: 15 minutes
Total cooking time: 55 minutes
Serves 8

1 cup (150 g) unsalted pistachio nuts
1/2 teaspoon ground cardamom
150 g unsalted butter, chopped
1 1/2 cups (185 g) self-raising flour
1 1/4 cups (310 g) caster sugar
3 eggs
1/2 cup (125 g) plain yoghurt
1 lime

1 Preheat the oven to moderate 180°C (350°F/Gas 4). Grease a 20 cm round cake tin and line the base with baking paper. Place the pistachios and cardamom in a food processor and pulse until just chopped. Add the butter, flour and 3/4 cup (185 g) of the caster sugar and pulse for 20 seconds, or until crumbly. Add the combined eggs and yoghurt and pulse for 10 seconds, or until just combined.

2 Spoon into the tin and smooth the surface. Bake for 45–50 minutes, or until a skewer comes out clean when inserted into the centre of the cake.

3 To make the syrup, peel the skin off the lime with a vegetable peeler—remove any white pith from the skin. Place the remaining caster sugar and 100 ml water in a small saucepan and stir over low heat until the sugar has dissolved. Bring to the boil, then add the lime peel and cook for 5 minutes. Strain and cool slightly. Pierce the cake with a few skewer holes and pour the hot syrup over the cooled cake.

NUTRITION PER SERVE
Fat 24 g; Protein 8 g; Carbohydrate 58 g; Dietary Fibre 2 g; Cholesterol 117.5 mg; 1990 kJ (475 cal)

1

2

3

PASSIONFRUIT AND RICOTTA CAKE

Preparation time: 10 minutes
Total cooking time: 1 hour
Serves 8

125 g unsalted butter, chopped
1/2 cup (125 g) caster sugar
1 1/2 cups (185 g) self-raising flour
3 eggs, lightly beaten
1 teaspoon vanilla essence
170 g can passionfruit pulp, strained of seeds
150 g ricotta, finely crumbled
icing sugar, to dust

1 Preheat the oven to moderate 180°C (350°F/Gas 4). Grease a 20 cm springform tin and line the base with baking paper. Place the butter, sugar and flour in a food processor and pulse for 15–20 seconds, or until crumbly.

2 Add the combined egg, vanilla essence and passionfruit pulp and pulse for a further 10–15 seconds, or until the mixture is just combined. Transfer to a bowl and gently fold in the ricotta.

3 Spoon the mixture into the prepared tin and bake for 1 hour, or until a skewer comes out clean when inserted into the centre of the cake. Leave in the tin for 10 minutes before turning out onto a wire rack to cool. Dust with the icing sugar and serve.

NUTRITION PER SERVE
Fat 17.5 g; Protein 7 g; Carbohydrate 33 g; Dietary Fibre 3 g; Cholesterol 116 mg; 1315 kJ (315 cal)

1

2

3

APPLE AND ALMOND CAKE

Preparation time: 15 minutes
Total cooking time: 40 minutes
Serves 6

185 g unsalted butter, chopped
3/4 cup (185 g) caster sugar
3 eggs
1 Granny Smith apple, peeled, cored and chopped
1/3 cup (30 g) coarsely chopped dried apples
1/4 cup (40 g) whole blanched almonds
2 cups (250 g) self-raising flour
1/3 cup (80 ml) milk

1 Preheat the oven to moderate 180°C (350°F/Gas 4). Grease and line the base of a deep 20 cm round tin. Place the butter, sugar and eggs in a food processor and pulse for 1 minute, or until the mixture is light and creamy.
2 Add the fresh and dried apples and the almonds and process for 15 seconds. Add the flour and milk and process for a further 20 seconds, or until the apple and almonds are finely chopped and the mixture is thick and almost smooth.
3 Pour the mixture into the prepared tin and smooth the surface. Bake for 40 minutes, or until a skewer comes out clean when inserted into the centre of the cake. Leave in the tin for 5 minutes before turning onto a wire rack to cool.

NUTRITION PER SERVE
Fat 33 g; Protein 9.5 g; Carbohydrate 67.5 g; Dietary Fibre 3 g; Cholesterol 169.5 mg; 2480 kJ (595 cal)

COOK'S FILE
Note: Top with Lemon glacé icing (see page 9) and decorate with coloured cachous, if desired.

1

2

3

BUTTERMILK CAKE WITH FRESH BERRIES

Preparation time: 10 minutes
Total cooking time: 50 minutes
Serves 8

110 g unsalted butter, softened
200 g caster sugar
4 egg yolks
200 ml buttermilk
$1\frac{2}{3}$ cups (210 g) self-raising flour
1 teaspoon baking powder
300 ml cream, whipped
150 g fresh berries (raspberries, blueberries)

1 Preheat the oven to moderate 180°C (350°F/Gas 4). Grease a 20 cm springform tin and line the base with baking paper. Pulse the butter, sugar and egg yolks in a food processor for 1 minute, or until light and creamy.

2 Add the buttemilk, sifted flour and baking powder and blend for 15 seconds, or until the mixture is smooth.

3 Pour the mixture into the tin. Bake for 50 minutes, or until a skewer comes out clean when inserted into the centre of the cake. Leave in the tin for 5 minutes before turning onto a wire rack to cool. To serve, spread the top of the cake with cream and arrange the fresh berries on top. If desired, dust with icing sugar.

NUTRITION PER SERVE
Fat 30.5 g; Protein 6 g; Carbohydrate 47 g; Dietary Fibre 0 g; Cholesterol 177 mg; 2010 kJ (480 cal)

COOK'S FILE
Note: This cake will sink slightly when cooled.
Variation: If you prefer, you can dust the cake with icing sugar and serve the cream and berries on the side.

1

2

3

ALMOND AND SEMOLINA CAKE

Preparation time: 15 minutes
Total cooking time: 1 hour
Serves 6

1 orange
1 cup (125 g) self-raising flour
2/3 cup (125 g) ground almonds
2/3 cup (85 g) fine semolina
125 g unsalted butter, chopped
1 cup (250 g) caster sugar
2 eggs, lightly beaten
1/2 cup (125 ml) milk

1 Preheat the oven to moderate 180°C (350°F/Gas 4). Grease a deep 20 cm round cake tin and line the base with baking paper.
2 Finely grate the orange to give 2 teaspoons of rind, then squeeze to give 1/4 cup (60 ml) juice. Place the flour, almonds, semolina, butter and sugar in a food processor and pulse for 20 seconds, or until fine and crumbly. Combine the egg, milk, orange juice and rind. Add to the food processor and blend for 10 seconds, or until combined.
3 Pour the mixture into the tin and smooth the surface. Bake for 1 hour, or until a skewer comes out clean when inserted into the centre of the cake. Leave the cake in the tin for 5 minutes before turning onto a wire rack to cool. Serve warm or cool.

NUTRITION PER SERVE
Fat 29.5 g; Protein 10 g; Carbohydrate 68 g; Dietary Fibre 2.5 g; Cholesterol 115 mg; 2365 kJ (565 cal)

COOK'S FILE
Notes: Decorate with an Orange glacé icing (see page 9).
Ground almonds and semolina give the raw mixture a rough texture and the cooked cake a slightly crunchy texture.
Storage: Keep for up to 2 days in an airtight container in a cool, dry place.

PEACH AND SOUR CREAM CAKE

Preparation time: 15 minutes
Total cooking time: 55 minutes
Serves 6–8

200 g unsalted butter, chopped
1 1/4 cups (230 g) lightly packed soft brown sugar
2 cups (250 g) self-raising flour
1/2 teaspoon bicarbonate of soda
3 eggs, lightly beaten
1/2 cup (125 g) sour cream
825 g can sliced peaches, drained and chopped
1 teaspoon ground cinnamon

1 Preheat the oven to moderate 180°C (350°F/Gas 4). Grease a 22 cm springform tin and line the base with baking paper. Place the butter and 3/4 cup (140 g) of the sugar in a food processor. Sift the flour and bicarbonate of soda together and add to the food processor. Pulse for 30 seconds, or until crumbly.

2 Add the combined egg and sour cream and pulse for 10 seconds, or until just combined. Transfer to a large bowl and fold in the chopped peaches. Spoon the stiff mixture into the tin and smooth the surface.

3 To make the topping, combine the cinnamon and remaining brown sugar and sprinkle evenly over the cake. Bake for 55 minutes, or until a skewer comes out clean when inserted into the centre of the cake—cover with foil towards the end if it starts to brown. Cool for 5 minutes before turning out onto a wire rack to cool. Best served warm with cream.

NUTRITION PER SERVE (8)
Fat 29 g; Protein 6.5 g; Carbohydrate 56.5 g; Dietary Fibre 2 g; Cholesterol 151 mg; 2120 kJ (505 cal)

1

2

3

BANANA UPSIDE-DOWN CAKE

Preparation time: 15 minutes
Total cooking time: 1 hour 5 minutes
Serves 8

125 g unsalted butter, chopped
1/3 cup (60 g) lightly packed soft brown sugar
3–4 large bananas, sliced on the diagonal
2 cups (250 g) self-raising flour, sifted
1 teaspoon baking powder
1/2 cup (125 g) caster sugar
2 eggs
1/2 cup (125 ml) milk

1 Preheat the oven to moderate 180°C (350°F/Gas 4). Grease a deep 20 cm round cake tin. Melt 50 g of the butter in a small saucepan over low heat, then pour over the base of the tin. Sprinkle the brown sugar evenly over the base, then arrange the bananas on top to completely cover.

2 Place the flour, baking powder and sugar in a food processor, and pulse to combine. Make a well in the centre. Melt the remaining butter in a pan over low heat. Remove from the heat and cool. Combine the eggs and milk in a small bowl. Add the combined butter and egg mixture to the flour and process until just combined—do not overmix.

3 Spoon the mixture over the bananas and smooth the surface. Bake for 1 hour, or until a skewer comes out clean when inserted into the centre of the cake. Leave in the tin for 15 minutes before turning onto a wire rack to cool.

NUTRITION PER SERVE
Fat 15.5 g; Protein 6 g; Carbohydrate 54.5 g; Dietary Fibre 2 g; Cholesterol 88.5 mg; 1570 kJ (375 cal)

1

2

3

HONEY PICNIC CAKE

Preparation time: 15 minutes
Total cooking time: 1 hour
Serves 8–10

300 g sour cream
3/4 cup (165 g) firmly packed soft brown sugar
1 egg
2 cups (300 g) wholemeal plain flour
1 teaspoon baking powder
3 tablespoons honey, warmed
1/2 cup (50 g) pecans, chopped

1 Preheat the oven to slow 150°C (300°F/Gas 2). Grease a 22 x 12 cm loaf tin and line the base and the two long sides with baking paper. Blend the sour cream, sugar and egg in a food processor until combined.
2 Add the flour and baking powder and process until well blended. Add the honey and process until mixed. Add the nuts and process just long enough for them to mix through.
3 Spoon into the prepared tin and bake for 1 hour, or until a skewer comes out clean when inserted into the centre of the cake. Leave in the tin for 15 minutes before turning out onto a wire rack to cool.

NUTRITION PER SERVE (10)
Fat 16.5 g; Protein 5.5 g; Carbohydrate 41 g; Dietary Fibre 4 g; Cholesterol 57.5 mg; 1380 kJ (330 cal)

COOK'S FILE
Note: This cake is delicious served plain or buttered.

1

2

3

CARROT AND PINEAPPLE CAKE

Preparation time: 15 minutes
Total cooking time: 1 hour
Serves 12

- 2 eggs
- 3/4 cup (140 g) lightly packed soft brown sugar
- 1/4 cup (60 ml) vegetable oil
- 1 cup (125 g) self-raising flour
- 1/2 teaspoon bicarbonate of soda
- 1 teaspoon ground nutmeg
- 450 g can crushed pineapple, well drained
- 1 1/2 cups (150 g) grated carrot

1 Preheat the oven to warm 160°C (315°F/Gas 2–3). Grease a 20 cm ring tin and line the base with baking paper. Blend the eggs and sugar in a food processor until combined. With the motor running, slowly pour in the oil.

2 Sift the flour, bicarbonate of soda and nutmeg into a large bowl. Add the pineapple and carrot and roughly mix together with a wooden spoon. Pour the egg mixture in all at once and mix until thoroughly combined.

3 Spoon into the prepared tin and bake for 1 hour, or until a skewer comes out clean when inserted into the centre of the cake. Leave in the tin for 5 minutes then turn out onto a wire rack to cool.

NUTRITION PER SERVE
Fat 6 g; Protein 3 g; Carbohydrate 20 g; Dietary Fibre 2.5 g; Cholesterol 30 mg; 595 kJ (140 cal)

COOK'S FILE
Note: Decorate with Orange glacé icing (see page 9).

1

2

3

DRESSED UP PACKET CAKES

VANILLA CAKE WITH WHITE CHOCOLATE AND RASPBERRIES

Preparation time: 15 minutes
Total cooking time: 35 minutes
Serves 8

510 g packet French vanilla cake mix
1/3 cup (80 ml) vegetable oil
3 eggs
100 g white chocolate, chopped
3 cups (750 ml) cream
2 tablespoons icing sugar, sifted
600 g fresh or frozen raspberries
3 tablespoons raspberry jam

1 Preheat the oven to moderate 180°C (350°F/Gas 4). Lightly grease two 20 cm shallow round cake tins and line each base with baking paper. Beat the cake mix, oil, eggs and 290 ml water in a large bowl with electric beaters on low for 30 seconds. Increase the speed to medium and beat for 2 minutes, then pour into the prepared tins. Bake for 30–35 minutes, or until a skewer comes out clean when inserted into the centre of each cake. Leave in the tins for 10 minutes before turning out onto a wire rack to cool. Meanwhile, place the chocolate in a heatproof bowl. Bring a saucepan of water to the boil, remove from the heat and sit the bowl over the saucepan—ensure the base of the bowl doesn't touch the water. Stir occasionally until the chocolate has melted. Pour onto a flat surface in a 4 cm wide strip, smooth the surface and allow to set. Shave off strips with a sharp knife or vegetable peeler.

2 Beat the cream in a large bowl with electric beaters until firm peaks form. Remove one third of the cream, then fold the icing sugar through the remaining two thirds. Lightly crush half the raspberries. Cut each cake in half horizontally and place the first layer on a serving plate. Spread with a third of the jam, a third of the unsweetened cream, then scatter with a third of the crushed raspberries. Continue layering the cake and fillings, finishing with a cake layer. Spread the sweetened cream over the cake, covering the top and sides—use a flat-bladed knife to smooth the surface, then run the knife up the sides to form a lined pattern around. Arrange the chocolate shavings in the centre of the cake, standing up to form a peak. Arrange the remaining whole raspberries around the rim of the cake, piling up around the chocolate.

NUTRITION PER SERVE
Fat 62 g; Protein 9 g; Carbohydrate 70.5 g; Dietary Fibre 5.5 g; Cholesterol 199 mg; 3605 kJ (860 cal)

COOK'S FILE
Note: If using frozen raspberries, defrost, then drain on paper towels to absorb any excess juices.

1

2

CHOCOLATE TRUFFLE CAKE

Preparation time: 15 minutes
Total cooking time: 45 minutes
Serves 8

340 g packet chocolate cake mix
2 eggs
2/3 cup (170 ml) milk
60 g unsalted butter, softened
300 g dark chocolate, chopped
150 g unsalted butter, softened, extra
8 Swiss dark chocolate balls

1 Preheat the oven to moderate 180°C (350°F/Gas 4). Grease a 20 cm round deep cake tin and line the base with baking paper. Cover the base of a shallow 18 cm round cake tin with foil and set aside. Beat the cake mix, eggs, milk and butter with electric beaters on low speed for 1 minute, or until combined. Beat on medium for 4 minutes. Spoon into the prepared tin and bake for 40–45 minutes, or until a skewer comes out clean when inserted into the centre of the cake. Leave in the tin for 5 minutes before turning out onto a wire rack to cool. Meanwhile, place the chocolate in a heatproof bowl. Bring a saucepan of water to the boil then remove the pan from the heat. Sit the bowl over the pan—ensure the base of the bowl doesn't touch the water. Stir occasionally until the chocolate has melted. Pour half the chocolate into the foil-lined tin and smooth the surface, then refrigerate until semi-set. Beat the extra butter with electric beaters until light and creamy. Add the remaining, slightly cooled chocolate and beat for 1 minute, or until smooth and combined. If the mixture is runny, refrigerate until it reaches spreading consistency. Remove the semi-set chocolate from the fridge and, using the point of a sharp knife, mark the chocolate into 8 wedges. Refrigerate until set.

2 Cut the cake in half horizontally and spread the bottom half with chocolate butter icing and top with the other layer of cake. Spread the remaining icing over the top and side of the cake using a flat-bladed knife. Arrange the chocolate balls around the rim of the cake. Remove the chocolate from the tin and carefully break into wedges. Rest a wedge against each truffle with the narrow end pointing towards the centre of the cake.

NUTRITION PER SERVE
Fat 41 g; Protein 7 g; Carbohydrate 64 g; Dietary Fibre 1.5 g; Cholesterol 115.5 mg; 2675 kJ (640 cal)

1

2

ORANGE FLOWER SPONGE

Preparation: 15 minutes
Total cooking time: 25 minutes
Serves 6

510 g packet French vanilla cake mix
1/3 cup (80 ml) vegetable oil
5 eggs
1 tablespoon orange flower water
11 g sachet gelatine powder
75 g caster sugar
1 cup (250 ml) cream
2 oranges

1 Preheat the oven to moderate 180°C (350°F/Gas 4). Grease and flour two 20 cm shallow round cake tins—shake out the excess flour. Beat the cake mix, oil, 3 eggs and 290 ml water in a bowl with electric beaters on low speed until combined. Add 2 teaspoons of the orange flower water, then beat on the highest speed for 5 minutes, or until well combined and smooth. Pour the mixture evenly into the prepared tins and bake for 20–25 minutes, or until a skewer comes out clean when inserted into the centre of each cake. Leave in the tins for 5 minutes before turning out onto a wire rack to cool.

2 Place 2 tablespoons water in a small bowl, then sprinkle the gelatine over the surface. Stand the bowl in a saucepan of boiling water, coming halfway up the bowl—turn off the heat and stir until dissolved. Beat the sugar and remaining eggs in a bowl with electric beaters until thick and creamy, then beat in the remaining orange flower water. Lightly whip the cream. Remove the gelatine from the heat. Squeeze the juice from 1 orange to make 3 tablespoons of juice, stir through the gelatine, then stir into the egg mixture. Fold in the whipped cream and chill until ready to assemble the cake—if the mixture sets too firmly, quickly beat with electric beaters before using.

3 To assemble, remove the skin and pith from the remaining orange, cut into slices, then in half. Place one sponge on a serving plate and spread with half the filling. Place the other sponge on top and spread with the remaining filling. Arrange the orange slices around the rim of the cake and garnish with a little orange zest. Chill before serving.

NUTRITION PER SERVE
Fat 42.5 g; Protein 11 g; Carbohydrate 80 g; Dietary Fibre 2.5 g; Cholesterol 208.5 mg; 3065 kJ (730 cal)

1

2

3

SICILIAN CAKE WITH CHOCOLATE FROSTING

Preparation time: 15 minutes + 10 minutes soaking
Total cooking time: 55 minutes
Serves 12

2–3 tablespoons very finely chopped mixed dried fruit
2–3 tablespoons Cointreau
590 g packet vanilla cake mix
3 eggs
500 g ricotta
50 g icing sugar
450 g good-quality dark chocolate
125 g unsalted butter, chilled and chopped

1 Preheat the oven to warm 160°C (315°F/Gas 2–3). Grease and flour a 22 x 12 cm loaf tin, shaking out the excess flour. Soak the fruit and liqueur in a small bowl for 10 minutes. Beat the cake mix, eggs and 1 cup (250 ml) water with electric beaters on low speed until combined. Increase to medium speed and beat for 2 minutes, or until well combined. Pour into the tin and bake for 45–50 minutes, or until a skewer comes out clean when inserted into the centre of the cake. Leave in the tin for 6–8 minutes before turning out onto a wire rack to cool.

2 To make the filling, beat the ricotta in a bowl with electric beaters, then gradually beat in the icing sugar for 2–3 minutes, or until smooth. Coarsely grate or chop 50 g of the chocolate and fold into the ricotta mixture with the dried fruits and liqueur. Break the remaining chocolate into small pieces and place in a heatproof bowl with the butter. Bring a saucepan of water to the boil, reduce to a simmer and place the bowl over the pan—ensure the base doesn't touch the water. Stir occasionally to ensure even melting. Remove the bowl from the heat and beat until glossy and cooled to spreading consistency.

3 To assemble the cake, cut a little off the top to level the surface, then slice the cake horizontally to form three layers. Place the base layer of cake on a serving plate, spread with half the ricotta mixture, then top with the centre piece of cake. Spread with the remaining ricotta mixture and top with the final layer of cake. Spread the chocolate icing over the top and sides of cake. Chill for up to a day before serving.

NUTRITION PER SERVE
Fat 29.5 g; Protein 10 g; Carbohydrate 63 g; Dietary Fibre 1.5 g; Cholesterol 92 mg; 2300 kJ (550 cal)

1

2

3

TIRAMISU CAKE

Preparation time: 15 minutes
Total cooking time: 40 minutes
Serves 6–8

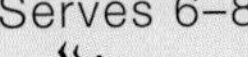

510 g packet French vanilla cake mix
3 eggs
1/3 cup (80 ml) vegetable oil
300 ml thick cream
1/4 cup (30 g) icing sugar
250 g mascarpone, chilled
100 ml Kahlua
1 1/2 tablespoons instant coffee

1 Preheat the oven to moderate 180°C (350°F/Gas 4). Grease a 22 cm square cake tin and line the base with baking paper. Beat the cake mix, eggs, oil and 290 ml water in a large bowl with electric beaters on low speed for 30 seconds. Increase the speed and beat for 2 minutes, or until well combined. Pour into the tin and bake for 35–40 minutes, or until a skewer comes out clean when inserted into the centre of the cake. Turn out onto a wire rack to cool. Beat the cream and sugar with a whisk until stiff. Fold in the mascarpone and 2 teaspoons of the Kahlua. Combine the coffee and the remaining Kahlua, stirring until the coffee has dissolved.

2 Cut the cake in half horizontally. Place the base of the cake on a serving plate and brush liberally with the coffee mixture, then spread one third of the cream mixture on top. Top with the other layer of cake and brush with the remaining coffee mixture. Spread the remaining cream mixture over the top and sides. If desired, sprinkle the surface with grated chocolate to serve.

NUTRITION PER SERVE (8)
Fat 41.5 g; Protein 9 g; Carbohydrate 60 g; Dietary Fibre 2 g; Cholesterol 142 mg; 2765 kJ (660 cal)

1

2

BUTTER CAKE WITH RASPBERRIES AND WHITE CHOCOLATE GANACHE

Preparation time: 15 minutes
Total cooking time: 35 minutes
Serves 8

340 g packet butter cake cake mix
2 eggs
2/3 cup (170 ml) milk
310 g unsalted soft butter, chopped
150 g white chocolate melts
130 g white chocolate, chopped
1 cup (250 ml) cream
150 g fresh or thawed, frozen raspberries

1 Preheat the oven to moderate 180°C (350°F/Gas 4). Grease a deep 20 cm round cake tin and line the base with baking paper. Beat the cake mix, eggs, milk and 60 g of the butter with electric beaters on low speed for 1 minute. Increase to medium speed and beat for a further 4 minutes. Spoon the mixture into the tin and bake for 35 minutes, or until a skewer comes out clean when inserted into the centre of the cake. Leave in the tin for 5 minutes before turning out onto a wire rack to cool completely.

2 To make the ganache, place the white chocolate melts, white chocolate, remaining butter and 1/2 cup (125 ml) of the cream in a saucepan. Stir over low heat until melted and smooth. Transfer the mixture to a bowl, cover with plastic wrap and leave to cool completely—do not refrigerate. Beat with electric beaters for 3–5 minutes, or until the ganache mixture is thick, pale and creamy.

3 Beat the remaining cream with electric beaters until stiff peaks form. Cut the cake in half horizontally. Place the bottom half on a serving plate and spread with the cream, then cover with three quarters of the raspberries. Top with the remaining half of cake and spread the top with the ganache, fluffing with a palate knife. Scatter the remaining raspberries on top and serve.

NUTRITION PER SERVE
Fat 63.5 g; Protein 8 g; Carbohydrate 54 g; Dietary Fibre 2 g; Cholesterol 196 mg; 3360 kJ (805 cal)

COOK'S FILE
Note: Cover the side of the cake with any leftover ganache.

1

2

3

QUICK BANANA BREAD

Preparation time: 10 minutes
Total cooking time: 55 minutes
Serves 12

250 g cream cheese, softened
1 cup (220 g) raw sugar
3 large ripe bananas, mashed (about 1 cup)
2 eggs, lightly beaten
300 g packet scone mix
1/2 cup (60 g) chopped pecans

1 Preheat the oven to moderate 180°C (350°F/Gas 4). Grease a 22 x 12 cm loaf tin and line the base and two long sides with a long sheet of baking paper. Beat the cream cheese and sugar in a large bowl with electric beaters until light and smooth. Add the banana and eggs and beat for 2 minutes, or until well combined. Fold in the scone mix and pecans until well combined.

2 Spoon into the prepared tin and smooth the surface. Bake for 40 minutes. Cover with foil and bake for a further 15 minutes, or until a skewer comes out clean when inserted into the centre of the cake. Leave in the tin for 10 minutes before turning out onto a wire rack to cool. Cool completely before serving.

NUTRITION PER SERVE
Fat 12.5 g; Protein 6.5 g; Carbohydrate 42 g; Dietary Fibre 2 g; Cholesterol 50.5 mg; 1265 kJ (305 cal)

COOK'S FILE
Note: This banana bread may be served with or without butter. It will keep well for up to 5 days stored in an airtight container.

1

2

QUICK BEESTING WITH MASCARPONE CREAM

Preparation time: 15 minutes
Total cooking time: 45 minutes
Serves 6–8

80 g unsalted butter, softened
1/4 cup (60 g) caster sugar
1/3 cup (40 g) slivered almonds, toasted
340 g packet golden butter cake mix
2 eggs, lightly beaten
3/4 cup (185 ml) milk
250 g mascarpone
2 tablespoons soft brown sugar

1 Preheat the oven to moderate 180°C (350°F/Gas 4). Grease a round 22 cm cake tin and line the base with baking paper. Melt 40 g of the butter in a small saucepan. Add the sugar and almonds and mix well. Spread the mixture evenly over the base of the prepared tin.

2 Beat the cake mix, egg, milk and remaining butter with electric beaters on low speed until combined. Increase to medium speed and beat for 4 minutes. Pour the mixture into the prepared tin and smooth the surface. Bake for 40 minutes, or until a skewer comes out clean when inserted in the centre of the cake. Leave in the tin for 10 minutes before turning out onto a wire rack to cool.

3 Stir the mascarpone and brown sugar together with a wooden spoon until well combined and chill before serving with the cake.

NUTRITION PER SERVE (8)
Fat 27.5 g; Protein 8 g; Carbohydrate 44 g; Dietary Fibre 1.5 g; Cholesterol 105 mg; 1880 kJ (450 cal)

COOK'S FILE
Note: If desired, dust the cake with icing sugar just before serving.

1

2

3

STRAWBERRY MOUSSE SPONGE

Preparation time: 15 minutes + 3 hours chilling
Total cooking time: 30 minutes
Serves 8

510 g packet French vanilla cake mix
3 eggs
1/3 cup (80 ml) vegetable oil
500 g fresh strawberries, hulled
1/4 cup (60 g) caster sugar
2 teaspoons powdered gelatine
1/2 cup (125 ml) cream
1 egg white

1 Preheat the oven to moderate 180°C (350°F/Gas 4). Grease two round 20 cm shallow cake tins and line each base with baking paper. Beat the cake mix, eggs, oil and 290 ml water with electric beaters on low speed for 30 seconds. Increase to medium speed and beat for 2 minutes, or until well combined. Evenly divide into the prepared tins and bake for 25–30 minutes, or until a skewer comes out clean when inserted into the centre of each cake. Leave in the tins for 5 minutes before turning out onto a wire rack to cool.

2 Place 250 g of the strawberries in a food processor and blend until smooth. Stir in the sugar. Pour the strawberry mixture into a saucepan and bring to the boil. Sprinkle in the gelatine, whisking until it has dissolved. Transfer to a bowl and set aside to cool. Slice half of the remaining strawberries—reserve the remaining whole strawberries to decorate the cake. Beat the cream to soft peaks. Beat the egg white in a clean bowl with electric beaters until soft peaks form. Fold one third of the cream into the cooled strawberry mixture, then fold in the egg white until combined.

3 Trim the top off one of the cakes to level the surface, then place on a serving plate. Fill with three quarters of the mousse and arrange the sliced strawberries on top. Spread the underside of the other cake with the remaining mousse so it will stick and place it on top. Spread the top of the cake with the remaining cream and decorate with the whole strawberries. Chill for 2–3 hours before serving.

NUTRITION PER SERVE
Fat 24 g; Protein 7.5 g; Carbohydrate 56.5 g; Dietary Fibre 3 g; Cholesterol 90 mg; 1950 kJ (465 cal)

1

2

3

COCONUT CAKE WITH COCONUT FROSTING

Preparation time: 15 minutes
Total cooking time: 40 minutes
Serves 8

340 g packet golden butter cake mix
2 eggs
60 g unsalted butter, softened
1 cup (250 ml) milk
1 1/3 cups (120 g) desiccated coconut
2 cups (250 g) icing sugar, sifted
1 egg white, lightly beaten
3/4 cup (45 g) shredded coconut, toasted

1 Preheat the oven to moderate 180°C (350°F/Gas 4). Lightly grease a 20 cm deep round cake tin and line the base with baking paper. Beat the cake mix, whole eggs, butter and 2/3 cup (170 ml) of the milk in a bowl with electric beaters on low speed for 1 minute, or until combined. Increase to medium speed and beat for 4 minutes. Fold in 1/3 cup (30 g) of the desiccated coconut. Spoon into the tin and bake for 40 minutes, or until a skewer comes out clean when inserted into the centre of the cake. Leave in the tin for 5 minutes before turning out onto a wire rack to cool. Cut in half horizontally.

2 To make the coconut frosting, place the icing sugar, egg white and remaining desiccated coconut in a small bowl. Mix to a paste, adding enough of the remaining milk to reach a good, spreadable consistency.

3 To assemble the cake, place the bottom layer on a serving plate and evenly spread with one third of the icing. Top with the other half of the cake and cover the top and side with the remaining icing using a flat-bladed knife, swirling to form a rough surface. Sprinkle with the shredded coconut, covering all side.

NUTRITION PER SERVE
Fat 25.5 g; Protein 6.5 g; Carbohydrate 66 g; Dietary Fibre 34 g; Cholesterol 69 mg; 2105 kJ (505 cal)

1

2

3

CHOCOLATE LAMINGTON BARS

Preparation time: 15 minutes
Total cooking time: 45 minutes
Serves 8–10

340 g packet rich chocolate cake mix
2 eggs
1 1/4 cups (310 ml) milk
2 cups (250 g) icing sugar, sifted
2 tablespoons cocoa powder
20 g unsalted butter, softened
1 1/4 cups (75 g) shredded coconut
1/2 cup (125 ml) thick cream, beaten until stiff

1 Preheat the oven to moderate 180°C (350°F/Gas 4). Grease two 25 x 7.5 cm bar tins and line each base with baking paper. Beat the cake mix, eggs and 1 cup (250 ml) of the milk with electric beaters on low speed until combined. Increase to medium speed and beat for 4 minutes. Pour the mixture into the prepared tins and smooth the surface. Bake for 40 minutes, or until a skewer comes out clean when inserted into the centre of the cakes. Leave in the tins for 5 minutes before turning out onto a wire rack to cool.

2 Sift the icing sugar and cocoa into a bowl. Add the butter and the remaining milk and mix to a smooth paste. Place the coconut on a baking tray and grill for 2 minutes—watch carefully so as not to burn. Toss and grill until golden. Leave to cool. Cut the cakes in half horizontally and spread each base with the cream. Cover with the top halves of cake. Spread the icing over the top and sides of each cake with a palette knife, then sprinkle all over with the shredded coconut.

NUTRITION PER SERVE (10)
Fat 17 g; Protein 5 g; Carbohydrate 52.5 g; Dietary Fibre 2 g; Cholesterol 60.5 mg; 1565 kJ (375 cal)

1

2

GLAZED APPLE CAKE

Preparation time: 15 minutes
Total cooking time: 50 minutes
Serves 6

2 small red apples
340 g packet golden butter cake mix
2 eggs
3/4 cup (185 ml) milk
60 g softened butter
2 teaspoons grated lemon rind
1/3 cup (105 g) apricot jam

1 Preheat the oven to moderate 180°C (350°F/Gas 4). Grease a 20 cm springform tin and line the base with baking paper. Peel and finely grate one apple. Cut the remaining unpeeled apple into quarters, core, then cut into thin slices. Beat the cake mix, eggs, milk, butter, lemon rind and grated apple with electric beaters on low speed until combined. Increase to medium speed and beat for 4 minutes. Pour the mixture into the prepared tin and bake for 40 minutes, or until a skewer comes out clean when inserted into the centre of the cake. Arrange the apple slices in a decorative pattern on the surface and bake for a further 10 minutes.

2 Heat the apricot jam in a small saucepan over low heat. Strain through a sieve to remove any lumps, then spread over the hot cake with a pastry brush. Leave in the tin for 10 minutes then remove to a wire rack to cool.

NUTRITION PER SERVE
Fat 16.5 g; Protein 6 g; Carbohydrate 59 g; Dietary Fibre 2 g; Cholesterol 91 mg; 1680 kJ (400 cal)

1

2

CHOCOLATE AND KAHLUA CAKE

Preparation time: 10 minutes
Total cooking time: 45 minutes
Serves 8–10

630 g packet chocolate cake mix
4 eggs
3/4 cup (185 ml) vegetable oil
1/2 cup (125 ml) Kahlua
1 cup (125 g) icing sugar
1/4 cup (60 ml) Kahlua, extra
chocolate-coated coffee beans, to decorate

1 Preheat the oven to moderate 180°C (350°F/Gas 4). Lightly grease a 2 litre kugelhopf tin. Beat the cake mix, eggs, oil, Kahlua and 1/4 cup (60 ml) water in a large bowl with electric beaters on medium speed for 3 minutes, or until smooth.
2 Spoon into the prepared tin and bake for 40–45 minutes, or until a skewer comes out clean when inserted into the cake. Leave in the tin for 10 minutes before turning out onto a wire rack to cool.
3 To make the glaze, place the icing sugar in a bowl and gradually stir in the extra Kahlua until smooth. Drizzle over the cooled cake, then sprinkle with coffee beans. Delicious served with whipped cream.

NUTRITION PER SERVE (10)
Fat 23 g; Protein 4.5 g; Carbohydrate 57 g; Dietary Fibre 1 g; Cholesterol 72.5 mg; 2000 kJ (475 cal)

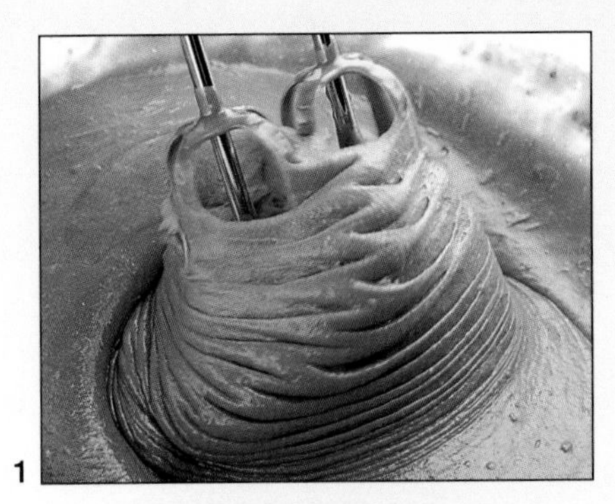
1

2

3

PRALINE BUTTER CAKE

Preparation time: 15 minutes
Total cooking time: 45 minutes
Serves 8

340 g packet butter cake mix
2 eggs
3/4 cup (185 ml) milk
60 g unsalted butter, softened
2/3 cup (110 g) macadamia nuts
1/2 cup (125 g) sugar
2 tablespoons brandy, or to taste
1 cup (250 ml) cream

1 Preheat the oven to moderate 180°C (350°F/Gas 4). Grease a deep 20 cm round cake tin and line the base with baking paper. Beat the cake mix, eggs, milk and butter with electric beaters on low speed until combined. Increase to medium speed and beat for 4 minutes. Pour into the prepared tin and bake for 40–45 minutes, or until a skewer comes out clean when inserted into the centre of the cake. Leave in the tin for 5 minutes before turning out onto a wire rack to cool.

2 Place the nuts in a frying pan over low heat until lightly toasted. Transfer to a foil-lined baking tray. Add the sugar to the pan with 1/4 cup (60 ml) water and stir over low heat until the sugar dissolves. Increase the heat and boil, without stirring, for 5 minutes, or until golden. Pour evenly over the macadamia nuts and allow to cool. Remove from the tray and reserve a large piece to garnish. Finely chop the remaining praline.

3 Cut the cake in half horizontally with a serrated knife. Drizzle 1 tablespoon of the brandy evenly over the cut surface of the cake. Turn the other half of cake upside-down and drizzle with the remaining brandy. Beat the cream to soft peaks, then fold in the finely chopped praline. Spread one third of the praline cream on the bottom half of the cake, then top with the other half. Spread the remaining praline cream on the top and around the side. Roughly break the reserved large piece of praline into smaller pieces and decorate the top of the cake.

NUTRITION PER SERVE
Fat 35.5 g; Protein 6 g; Carbohydrate 49.5 g; Dietary Fibre 1.5 g; Cholesterol 110.5 mg; 2255 kJ (540 cal)

1

2

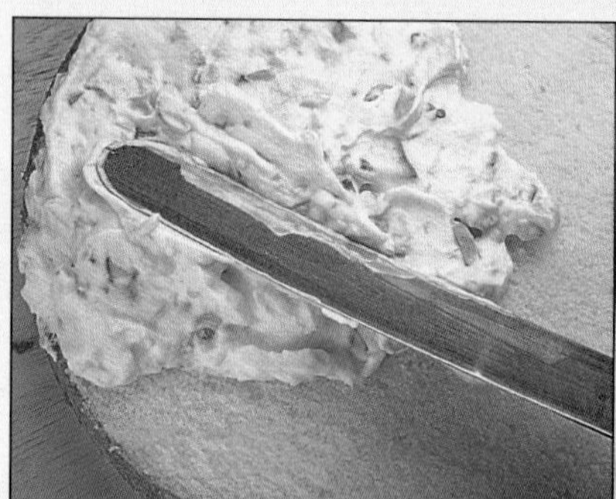
3

PASSIONFRUIT BUTTER CAKE

Preparation time: 15 minutes
Total cooking time: 25 minutes
Serves 8

1 cup (60 g) shredded coconut
340 g packet butter cake mix
2 eggs
40 g unsalted butter
1 cup (125 g) icing sugar, sifted
1–2 tablespoons passionfruit pulp (about 1 fresh passionfruit)
200 ml thick cream

1 Preheat the oven to moderate 180°C (350°F/Gas 4). Grease two round 20 cm shallow cake tins and line each base with baking paper. Spread the coconut on a baking tray and cook for 5–10 minutes, or until lightly golden. Leave to cool. Beat the cake mix, eggs, 30 g of the butter and 1/2 cup (125 ml) cold water in a large bowl with electric beaters on low speed for 1 minute. Increase to medium speed and beat for 4 minutes. Pour into the prepared tins and bake for 20–25 minutes, or until a skewer comes out clean when inserted into the centre of the cakes. Leave in the tins for 5 minutes before turning out onto a wire rack to cool.

2 To make the icing, place the icing sugar, passionfruit pulp, remaining butter and 1 tablespoon boiling water in a bowl and mix well. Beat the cream until soft peaks form.

3 Trim the top of one of the cakes to level the surface. Place on a serving plate and spread half the cream over the surface. Place the other cake on top, then spread the remaining cream around the side. Press the toasted coconut around the side of the cake and cover the top with the icing.

NUTRITION PER SERVE
Fat 23 g; Protein 4.5 g; Carbohydrate 48.5 g; Dietary Fibre 2 g; Cholesterol 87.5 mg; 1725 kJ (410 cal)

1

2

3

CARAMEL BUTTER CAKE

Preparation time: 15 minutes
Total cooking ime: 50 minutes
Serves 8–10

340 g packet butter cake mix
2 eggs
3/4 cup (185 ml) milk
185 g unsalted butter, softened
140 g caramel chocolate buds
1/4 cup (60 ml) cream
55 g chocolate coated finger biscuits (24 biscuits)

1 Preheat the oven to moderate 180°C (350°F/Gas 4). Grease a deep 20 cm round cake tin and line the base with baking paper. Beat the cake mix, eggs, milk and 60 g of the butter with electric beaters on low speed for 1 minute. Increase to medium speed and beat for 4 minutes. Pour into the tin and smooth the surface. Bake for 40–45 minutes, or until a skewer comes out clean when inserted into the centre of the cake. Leave in the tin for 5 minutes before turning out onto a wire rack to cool.

2 To make the chocolate ganache, place the chocolate buds, cream and remaining butter in a saucepan and stir over low heat until melted and smooth. Transfer to a bowl and leave to cool—do not refrigerate. Beat with electric beaters for 3 minutes, or until thick, pale and creamy.

3 Cut the cake in half horizontally. Place the bottom half of the cake on a serving plate and spread with one third of the ganache, then top with the other half of the cake. Cover the whole cake with the remaining ganache. Place the biscuits in a zigzag pattern around the side of the cake. Decorate with coloured cachous, if desired.

NUTRITION PER SERVE (10)
Fat 28 g; Protein 5 g; Carbohydrate 38 g; Dietary Fibre 1 g; Cholesterol 97 mg; 1755 kJ (420 cal)

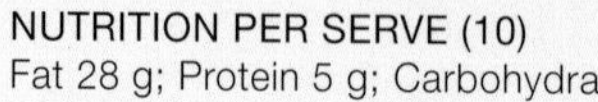

1

2

3

BLACK FOREST CAKE

Preparation time: 15 minutes
Total cooking time: 45 minutes
Serves 8–10

510 g packet chocolate fudge cake mix
3 eggs
1/3 cup (80 ml) vegetable oil
200 g dark chocolate, chopped
250 g unsalted butter, softened
1 1/4 cups (310 ml) cream, whipped
680 g jar pitted morello cherries, drained

1 Preheat the oven to moderate 180°C (350°F/Gas 4). Grease two 20 cm round shallow cake tins and line the bases with baking paper. Beat the cake mix, eggs, oil and 1 1/4 cups (310 ml) water in a large bowl with electric beaters for 30 seconds. Increase to medium speed and beat for 2 minutes. Pour evenly into the tins and bake for 40–45 minutes, or until a skewer comes out clean when inserted into the centre of the cake.

2 Place the chocolate in a heatproof bowl. Bring a saucepan of water to the boil, remove from the heat and sit the bowl over the saucepan—ensure the base doesn't touch the water. Stir occasionally until the chocolate has melted. Cool slightly. Beat the butter in a bowl with electric beaters until light and creamy. Add the chocolate, beating for 1 minute, or until smooth and well combined. If the mixture is too runny, refrigerate until it reaches a spreading consistency.

3 Cut each cake in half horizontally and place the first layer on a serving plate. Spread the cake evenly with one third of the whipped cream and top with one quarter of the cherries. Continue layering with the remaining cake and filling ingredients, finishing with the cake on top. Spread the chocolate cream over the top and side of the cake with a flat-bladed knife. Pile the remaining cherries in the centre of the cake and serve.

NUTRITION PER SERVE (10)
Fat 54 g; Protein 6.5 g; Carbohydrate 57 g; Dietary Fibre 2 g; Cholesterol 161 mg; 3045 kJ (725 cal)

1

2

3

LEMON BLUEBERRY BUTTER CAKE

Preparation time: 15 minutes
Total cooking time: 45 minutes
Serves 8

- 340 g packet butter cake mix
- 2 eggs
- 3/4 cup (185 ml) milk
- 60 g unsalted butter, softened
- 2 teaspoons finely grated lemon rind
- 1/2 cup (125 ml) cream
- 2 tablespoons purchased lemon butter
- 150 g fresh blueberries

1 Preheat the oven to moderate 180°C (350°F/Gas 4). Lightly grease a deep 20 cm round cake tin and line the base with baking paper. Beat the cake mix, eggs, milk, butter and lemon rind with electric beaters on low speed until combined. Increase to medium speed and beat for 4 minutes. Spoon into the prepared tin and smooth the surface. Bake for 40–45 minutes, or until a skewer comes out clean when inserted into the centre of the cake. Leave in the tin for 5 minutes before turning out onto a wire rack to cool. Cut the cake in half horizontally with a serrated knife.

2 Beat the cream and lemon butter together with electric beaters until soft peaks form. Spread the lemon cream mixture over the base of the cake.

3 Arrange the blueberries on the lemon cream, then gently place the remaining cake on top. If desired, dust the cake with icing sugar before serving.

NUTRITION PER SERVE
Fat 18.5 g; Protein 5 g; Carbohydrate 38.5 g; Dietary Fibre 1.5 g; Cholesterol 87.5 mg; 1405 kJ (335 cal)

1

2

3

INDEX

INTERNATIONAL GLOSSARY OF INGREDIENTS

bicarbonate of soda	baking soda
caster sugar	superfine sugar
choc bits	chocolate chips
dark chocolate	semi-sweet chocolate
desiccated coconut	shredded coconut
French vanilla cake mix	Victorian sponge mix
icing sugar	confectioners' sugar
plain flour	all-purpose flour
self-raising flour	self-rising flour
thick cream	double cream

Published by Murdoch Books®, a division of Murdoch Magazines Pty Limited, GPO Box 1203, Sydney NSW 1045.

Managing Editor: Rachel Carter **Editor:** Stephanie Kistner **Creative Director:** Marylouise Brammer **Designer:** Norman Baptista **Food Director:** Jane Lawson **Food Editor:** Rebecca Clancy **Recipe Development:** Ruth Armstrong, Rebecca Clancy, Michelle Earl, Jo Glynn, Jane Griffiths, Barbara Lowery, Dianna McLean, Kate Murdoch, Christine Osmond, Sally Parker, Anna Phillips, Melita Smilovic, Angela Tregonning **Home Economists:** Alison Adams, Justin Finlay, Valli Little, Evelyn Morris, Fiona Skinner **Photographers:** Tony Lyons, Rob Reichenfeld, Reg Morrison (steps) **Food Stylist:** Cherise Koch, Mary Harris **Food Preparation:** Briget Palmer, Jo Glynn, Renee Aiken (steps) **UK Consultant:** Maggi Altham **Nutritionist:** Dr Susanna Holt. **Chief Executive:** Mark Smith **Publisher:** Kay Scarlett.

The nutritional information provided for each recipe does not include any garnishes or accompaniments, such as rice, unless they are included in specific quantities in the ingredients. The values are approximations and can be affected by biological and seasonal variations in food, the unknown composition of some manufactured foods and uncertainty in the dietary database. Nutrient data given are derived primarily from the NUTTAB95 database produced by the Australian New Zealand Food Authority.

National Library of Australia Cataloguing-in-Publication Data. Quick and easy cakes. Includes index. ISBN 1 74045 059 0. 1. Cake. 641.8653. First printed 2001. Printed by PMP PRINT.